MW01233544

THE WHITEWATER TIDAL WAVE

EVERY AMERICAN TAXPAYER IS AFFECTED!

A.K. Karsky

Copies of softcover editions available
by mail order directly from the publisher.
Retail price: $7.95, plus $3.00 S&H
or order through your favorite bookstore.

Printed in the United States of America.

A.K. Karsky

Copyright © 1995
ISBN #1-883740-25-8
Library of Congress Card Number: 93-096477

Cover Design
Foster & Foster, Inc.

Cover Cartoon
Glen Bernhardt
Copyright © 1995

All rights reserved. No part of this book may be reproduced or transmitted in any form or by any means, electronic, or mechanical, including photocopying, recording, or by any information storage or retrieval system, without permission in writing from the publisher.

Publisher
Pebble Beach Press, Ltd.
P.O. Box 1171
Pebble Beach, CA 93953
Tel: 408-372-5559   Fax: 408-375-4525

This book is dedicated to
the American Taxpayers who keep
right on paying and trusting in the
good ol' U.S.A., even though they know
she is cheating on them constantly.
God Bless them!
May common sense return
to America.

Table of Contents

Part I

Why the "Whitewater" Hearings?

There are many reasons. The only one that is important to you as an American taxpayer is that there is a crisis in the U.S.A. and "Whitewater" is at the bottom of that crisis. The Republicans would like to get rid of Clinton for good. The question is: Do they have the guts and determination to impeach the President of the United States of America? After you finish this book, you will be anxious to help them do their jobs. If you and everyone else participates, we can control the crisis. If it can be proven, the information that is available, some of which is compiled in this book, is certainly enough to do that and more. The charges that may be brought against Bill and Hillary Clinton are extremely serious; if not devastating to not only them, but to our whole nation and perhaps the world. <u>Every American taxpayer is affected</u>!

Remember while you read this book and follow the hearings, our Judicial System assumes that we are innocent until proven guilty. We, therefore, have to be absolutely certain, by an overwhelming amount of evidence, that anyone accused of a serious crime be proven guilty beyond a reasonable doubt. This applies to you and me, O.J. Simpson and even the President of the United States of America.

The Senate Banking Committee and the House Committee on Banking must rise above the self-serving interest of the banks. Already Senator D'Amato and Congressman Leach, who chair these committees, are soft peddling the "Whitewater" accusations. Why? Because the banks told them that we will have a world-wide monetary crisis if Clinton is impeached. D'Amato and Leach must be brought to face the responsibility that we placed in them. The banks and insurance companies, in effect, control the United States. The Federal Reserve and our monetary system is about to collapse. It is held together artificially by a combination of the above power structures with media mirrors and Wall Street hype. If left to its own devices, the power of that combination will cheat us of the truth about "Whitewater". Every American taxpayer must get persuasively involved to protect him or herself from the tyranny of the "Establishment".

The American people elected D'Amato and Leach, not the banks. The American people must know the truth, we do not want the "business as usual" treatment to "save face". Full disclosure is what Americans want. Full disclosure is what Americans must insist upon. Full disclosure is what Americans must get. Let's go for it! No more government cover-ups!"

What is "Whitewater" all about?

The current generation in America has been trained in the art of real estate deals on "Dallas" and "Dynasty". "Whitewater" tops anything that J.R. Ewing or Alexis Carrington Colby ever pulled off. You have to pay close attention to this scam to understand it. We wish that it was funny and we could joke about it. However, the American

2

taxpayers, are the suckers. There is nothing to laugh about. We, our children and grandchildren will all be paying for it. "Whitewater" is a small part of how we got cheated, by con men, out of several hundred billion dollars in the 1980's. Arkansas was a perfect environment to pull it off. It's a classic lesson on how to make three million dollars developing a remote tract of land without selling one square foot of it. It's sort of a high stakes welfare program. You do nothing and eventually, the government takes care of everything.

Liberal democrats have been preaching this kind of socialism since time began. You and I have been paying, so they could have fun playing. The game is called "Let's change society". However, it's time to realize that we can't afford that game anymore and never could! Now, their champ, our "President", is under investigation. Was he practicing what he preached? Some people say "Yeah, and how!" Did he get away with too much? -- Did we let him? Do we get away with too much? Those questions we have to ask ourselves.

Perhaps the pain and suffering we all felt as a result of O.J. Simpson's apparent downfall was a test for our culture? I don't know about you, but O.J. was a hero to a lot of Americans. The phenomenon of his trial and the fact that some of us can't bear to let go of that image he portrayed will be magnified tremendously if and when our president goes on trial. For our own sake, we should hope both are found innocent.

Depression is a terrible state of mind. It is self-inflicted and destructive to our soul. Anger, on the other hand, releases that depressed sensation and is a sort of grief that allows a more sane survival. When you are finished with this book, I hope you have been provoked into anger and into action as a result of your anger. If you get depressed, then promise yourself that you will read it again and again, until you get angry. "Mad as Hell", then we can all survive.

Ready? Here we go!

First, you find some cheap dirt, in the boondocks preferably. In the "Whitewater" case, there were 230 acres in the Ozarks, along the White River, priced at $90,000. It was over forty miles to the nearest grocery store. Now you need some friends and partners. Your number one friend is an appraiser. Equally important is your friendly banker. As you may imagine, Arkansas was full of friendly appraisers, bankers, etc..., etc....

Your friendly appraiser does a glowing appraisal because you tell him you are marketing extremely desirable home sites along river frontage. (Leave out the stuff about the flooding; after all, the Army Corps of Engineers has all of that information. It's public record if someone wants to know.)

Let's say the appraiser certifies the value at $180,000. The friendly banker can go up to 80 percent of value by regulations. So, you "max-out" a loan for $144,000, buy the property with $90,000 (perhaps you can get a cash discount), pay the costs of say $4,000, and you pocket at least $50,000, depending on how good a negotiator you are.

Now you are a bona fide real estate developer without even an MBA from Harvard.

The next step is you have to spend some of the bank's money to get really rich. Take $10,000 and subdivide, bulldoze a road to the property, and cut down some trees so it looks like a bunch of ready to build lots. Do it so you maximize the views of that river. If the governor is in on the deal and you know the ropes, get the state to spend $150,000 on a two mile access road from the highway to "paradise". The governor justifies the state's contribution by imposing higher taxes on your neighbors. In his next campaign he can say he created jobs building roads.

Once that is done, do a little marketing brochure. Hire a professional photographer, have him take some fantastic pictures of the trees turning color, and of the quiet river gently flowing by the banks. This new luxury estate community is a great place to raise kids. Then, call up your friendly appraiser and he revaluates your property at $500,000. Call you friendly banker immediately and go on over to get your refinancing at 80 percent of $500,000 or $400,000. Pay off the other loan and you have approximately a quarter of a million dollars in your pocket.

Now you're ready to graduate to a new level of enterprise in the U.S.A.: You become a builder! How? Don't go out and buy lumber, nails, hammers, etc..., if you do that, you may get some callouses on your hands. Just get a couple of stock plans from the friendly blue printer, The Bungalowcraft Company. Make a few phony sales of homesites with those plans to some of your friends.

5

Wow! Now you have recorded sales in the county recorder's office. You might as well set-up an escrow company. Why let some poor slob make the money on escrows when you can get it?

Get that friendly appraiser back again and hustle on down to that bank in your new Mercedes, with the cellular phone in it, just like the "big boys". Get your new loan for $1,500,000 and do a "land flip", selling the whole thing to Company "A" for $2,250,000, which sells it to Company "B" for $2,900,000, which sells it back to your company for $3,800,000. Quick! Borrow 80 percent of $3,800,000 or approximately $3,000,000 and put it in your pocket or hide it somewhere. Now you are a bona fide millionaire, builder and developer, all with other people's money. Unfortunately for us, it turns out to be our money, the taxpayers' money. The "Whitewater" loans actually totaled over $3,000,000. There is nothing wrong with running up the value of land from $90,000 to $3,000,000. That's not the problem. The problem surfaces when no one buys those lots at that price because the market is not there and the developer can not pay back the loan. We paid it back. Whitewater Development Company did not. Ask--who kept the change?

This is what <u>Whitewater Development Company</u> and <u>Madison Guarantee Savings & Loan</u> apparently were all about. It is reported that "Whitewater" figures, David Hale and Dean Paul, once flipped "Castle Grande", another project, back and forth from $200,000 to $825,000 all in one day. "Castle Grande" began with a $75,000 piece of swamp land. Eventually they ran it up to $3,000,000, of which they borrowed 80 percent, or $2,400,000, without building a thing. Later on Governor

6

Jim Guy Tucker and Steve Smith developed what they called "Campobello". It started with $150,000, and they parlayed it to $4,000,000 in less than two years.

Finally, when you refuse to make your loan payments, and when you can't borrow more, call your friendly lawyer, after you stash some money in a secret Swiss bank account and say the magic words, "Chapter 11 of the Bankruptcy Code" for your company and Whitewater Development Corporation and thousands of others like it. The bank has to eat your loan. The money is all gone. Record keeping is poor; your friendly accountant takes care of all that. Be careful about tax losses though, that's double dipping and jail if you go that far. Don't feel sorry for the bankers. Don't even worry; the FDIC will take care of it. The Federal Deposit Insurance Corporation was made just for that. One day you wake up when President Reagan announced that the Savings & Loans have collapsed, but everything is cool. The Resolution Trust Corporation (R.T.C.) has been formed to take care of the problem. Reported estimates of the taxpayers losses are only sixty billion dollars, at this time, but not to worry, everything is insured in the good ol' U.S.A. What he doesn't say is: How you and I got into this deal. All of a sudden, the insurance company is you and me. Why didn't we collect any premiums? We should have. All other insurance premiums are paid to the insurance company. Why not ours? Who wrote that policy and signed our names to it? Is this how democracy works?

Did this really happen? If the Republicans want Bill Clinton's hide bad enough, you bet it happened and it may be proven at the "Whitewater" Hearings. Bill Clinton and Hillary, with their partner, Jim McDougal, may have taken several million dollars from the Small Business Administration and several banks and savings & loans, including the Bank of Kingston.

Madison Guarantee Savings & Loan was the worst of the bunch in Arkansas. Their books, if exposed, we are told, will show at that time, millions of dollars of 24 hour brokeraged deposits and over seventeen million dollars in insider loans. A brokeraged deposit, in case you are curious, is a way to build up your overnight assets so you look good as an S&L at the end of every day. The trouble is, it's an inverted pyramid. Let's say you are the broker and I am the S&L. I solicit you to bring your deposits and I agree to pay you a broker's commission each time you bring a deposit. We agree to split the commission under the table. You bring in one million a day, leave it for 24 hours and you and I split $10,000 per day. Do it again the next day, and the next, and the next, keep going until --- oops---, we got caught. It only takes a hundred $10,000 commissions and the million is gone. Then what?

Whitewater Development Corporation appeared sincere. It showed T.V. commercials starring Jim McDougal's beautiful wife, Susan, riding a horse on the property. Others showed her riding around the property in Bill Clinton's restored '67 Mustang. After "Whitewater" broke, the deals stopped. The R.T.C. criminal referral that Bill Clinton suppressed shows corporations such as Smith - Tucker - McDougal, Tucker - Smith - McDougal, McDougal-Smith -Tucker, and Smith-McDougal. Clever, eh? That's what MBA's and Rhodes scholars can do for you, if you are lucky enough to be able to hire them.

Part II

Probable Accusations:

The information presented in this volume goes beyond the "Whitewater" incident. It has been compiled and researched from over one thousand articles in the print media, the public record, letters, writings, from people, such as mentioned previously, and others who asked that their names not be revealed because they feared for their life.

The accusations against our President are unthinkable. What Bill Clinton and Hillary are accused of will make most of us question the sanity of the accuser. Unfortunately for us, we have been conditioned to "hear no evil, see no evil, speak no evil". That is evil's way of getting away with murder, literally. Most of us are not ready to believe that our president may be a killer, a drug king, a rapist, an adulterer, and that he may have committed other felonies. Let's hope and pray he is none of the above.

Pebble Beach Press, Ltd. has decided to print this volatile information as it was obtained. It may not be complete, there may be more. The American taxpayer and the people of the world ought to know what is possibly facing them. Undoubtedly, some of this information will be disclosed during the televised hearings. It is provided here for the American and foreign T.V. viewer as a book for easy reference. The text is followed by a list of characters who will be or have been the players in this terrible nightmare. There is no doubt that "The

Whitewater Tidal Wave" will affect every man, woman and child living on this planet. This is your opportunity to participate, as you have on radio and television talk shows. This time in writing, to your congressman and senator, to Senator D'Amato and Congressman Leach, directly. Then see what happens and follow this book while the hearings are on the air. You will have inside information. It's kind of like knowing the game plan at the Super Bowl and seeing if the coaches and players can carry it out.

Charges which may be brought against the Clintons:

- Election Fraud
- Obstruction of Justice
- Rape & Adultery
- Murder of over 20 people
- Drug Running & Money Laundering
- Bank Fraud
- Insider Trading
- Witness Tampering
- Destruction of Subpoenaed Documents

The most serious accusation may be that Bill Clinton, President of the United States of America, or his cronies, had over twenty people murdered by hired assassins. These victims may have known too much or were witnesses who became an embarrassment to President

Clinton. All of them may have known about or may have been included in scandals that may be exposed at the "Whitewater" Hearings. The information contained in this book was provided by people who wrote about, talked about, witnessed, and spent over eighteen years in Arkansas and personally knew the Clintons, along with Jim McDougal, Vince Foster and many others you will hear about during the hearings.

So far, there have been numerous indictments handed down by the Little Rock County Grand Jury. More indictments are on the way. It has been reported that Hillary has been calling home and telling friends that the Clintons will be moving back to Little Rock before the year is out. The question is, "Will the Whitewater Tidal Wave get 'Slick Willy' and Hillary?"

Recently, five felony charges have been filed against Neal T. Ainley, President of Perry County Bank. He is charged with federal law violations in a conspiracy that involved "concealing from the IRS, and others, the withdrawal of large amounts of U.S. currency during the 1990 Clinton Campaign". Bruce Lindsey, now a top White House aide, who was Clinton's campaign treasurer at the time, has just been indicted. The indictment charges that the conspiracy involved "others, known and unknown". It mentions "various overt acts" were involved in the "furtherance of the conspiracy". Apparently, Ainley personally delivered the cash to Lindsay, for use in the 1990 Clinton campaign.

Published reports have said that the investigation is centered on the relationship of this small bank headed by a longtime friend of Clinton's and appointee to the State

Highway Commission, Herby Branscum, Jr.

You have probably never heard of Luther "Jerry" Parks before; but remember his name.

> - "They had my father killed to save Bill Clinton's political career."

> - "He threatened Clinton, saying he'd go public if he didn't get his money."

The above quotations are from the London Sunday Telegraph. The first quote is by Gary Parks, the second by his mother, Jane.

What apparently happened is this: the Parks owned a business, which supplied guards for Clinton's presidential campaign and transition headquarters. Jerry Parks was in charge of security and he knew a lot about what was going on. For six years, while Clinton was Governor, Jerry compiled information on Clinton's sexual escapades. Clinton owed him a lot of money for past services but refused to pay.

A few days before Jerry was killed, his home was ransacked, his files were taken, photos and negatives destroyed... a security alarm system was cut, by experts, according to his wife, Jane.

On September 23, 1993, after a dinner meeting in a Little Rock restaurant, Luther "Jerry" Parks, driving on his way home, was apparently stopped by some men. Later that night, nine bullets were extracted from Jerry's body by the county coroner. Witnesses said that nine shots were fired into Jerry's car at point blank range by the men who stopped him.

Most of the information we are presenting sounds like "tabloid trash". The sad truth is that the people who are involved in "Whitewater" are unfortunately, apparently nothing but trash. It isn't surprising, today trash is abundant everywhere, including the White House.

At midnight, January 24, 1994, on the fourteenth floor of the Worthen Tower, in the Little Rock offices of Pete Marwick, a fire took place. It may be brought up at the hearings that this fire consumed the records of what was reported to be Pete Marwick's audit of Madison Guarantee Savings & Loan.

A former Pete Marwick executive tells that word came down from Clinton himself, to destroy that evidence. This fire occurred just after Robert Fiske started as "Whitewater" investigator. If true, Clinton obviously learned a lesson from President Nixon's mistake.

The hearings might reveal that the medical records Bill Clinton refused to release were also torched in his doctor's office. You will find that witnesses, if called, may testify that the "allergies" "Slick Willy" didn't want us to know about were in fact destroyed nasal passages, destroyed by snorting cocaine.

Dan Lasater, one of Bill's best friends, is a convicted cocaine dealer. He employed Bill's brother, Roger, at Lasater & Company, which issued over one billion dollars of Arkansas State Bonds in the 1980's. The hearings may reveal that the beneficiaries of each bond were required to make a substantial donation to Clinton.

Both Clinton and Lasater were flying high in Lasater's private jet, some reports called it "a cocaine laden jet". The hearings may bring out even more about the Clinton/Lasater junkets. There are unconfirmed reports that witnesses may be called to testify about wild parties hosted by young girls, at which "blizzards of cocaine" were going down.

We are told that Roger Clinton admitted doing six to eight grams per day, and he admitted to being a dealer for Lasater. We will never know how much Bill used, but Sally Perdue, a former Miss Arkansas, and Talk Show Hostess, told the London Sunday Telegraph that in 1983, while she was having an affair with Governor Clinton, Bill would smoke two or three ready-made joints drawn from his cigarette case in a typical evening. She added that yes, he inhaled, and on occasion he pulled out a baggie of cocaine and prepared a "line" right on her table.

The hearings might also bring out that Lasater laundered hundreds of millions of drug dollars through his firm. Dan Lasater went to prison after his conviction, six months later, his friend Bill Clinton pardoned him. While Lasater was still in prison he turned his company over to Patsy Thomasson, one of Bill's top administrative aides. Governor Clinton then continued to funnel all the state's bonds through the company. Then, she got six hundred sixty million dollars in Arkansas State Bonds for Lasater's company. Lasater & Company was the major source of brokered deposits in Madison Guarantee

Savings & Loan. Now Patsy works at the White House!

We understand that Janet Reno, U.S. Attorney General, is holding Bill Clinton's personal drug supplier in Leavenworth Prison, incommunicado. Many people will speak out. The word is that half of Arkansas will try to get their names in the headlines by volunteering as witnesses. The other half will volunteer as jurors.

Jon Parnell Walker's friends, family and co-workers, all agreed on one thing: he was not depressed and he was not suicidal. Yet one day, Jon's body was found at the bottom of the multi-story Lincoln Towers Apartments in Arlington, Virginia. He just moved there from Kansas City. It was reported by the press that Jon had decided to suddenly climb over the balcony railing and jump.

You see, Jon Parnell Walker was a "Senior Investigator Specialist" with the Resolution Trust Corporation, which investigates and disposes of failed savings & loans.

Jon Parnell Walker was getting close to exposing the scam. He had the investigation moved to Washington, D.C. and he was killed shortly thereafter. His name should come up in the hearings. His family will talk.

As we pointed out earlier, Whitewater Development Corporation borrowed millions of dollars from Madison Guarantee Savings & Loan, which eventually went bankrupt. You and I, and other American taxpayers, paid sixty-five million dollars to bail it out because apparently Jim McDougal, the Clintons and others made millions of dollars at our expense.

15

Kathy Ferguson, 38, was the wife of Danny Ferguson. You may remember, he was the Arkansas patrolman who said he brought Paula Jones to Bill Clinton's hotel room.

- On May 10, 1993, Kathy was found dead with a pistol in her hand. "A suicide", said the police.

However, this is what may come out at the hearings.

Apparently, Kathy talked a lot about such things. She gossiped about how her husband was forced to bring women to Bill Clinton, and how Bill made him stand watch while he had sex. She said Bill Clinton had hundreds of women brought to him, several per day, young, pretty women, pulled over for speeding, or other traffic violations, who apparently would be given a choice between a jail sentence or a sexual encounter with the governor.

According to Kathy, part of Danny's job was to make sure that each woman was ready and willing when Bill met her. Kathy told people about how mad Bill Clinton got when Paula Jones refused his advances. She said, "Bill hates rejection".

Kathy divorced Danny. She took a new boyfriend, Bill Shelton, an Arkansas Police Officer. He was openly critical about the suicide story of his girlfriend. He complained to the authorities. However, about a month after Kathy died, he was found dead on top of her grave. His death was also called a suicide.

Perhaps we will find out exactly how both of them died at the "Whitewater" Hearings. In the meantime, consider the following facts about Kathy's death:

- Nurses, if they want to commit suicide, don't use guns. Kathy was a nurse. She had access and knew the lethal doses of many medications.

- Women generally never use guns to kill themselves.

- Kathy's co-workers at Baptist Memorial Hospital in Little Rock, all agree that Kathy Ferguson would never kill herself. They will testify if called upon.

Several weeks after that, Danny reversed his story, retracting his comments about bringing Paula Jones to Clinton. These names should be big in the hearings, watch for them.

The Vince Foster situation will be among the most difficult for Bill and Hillary to overcome. It's difficult to believe that Vince Foster killed himself. Normal procedures after an incident such as Foster's untimely death are to seal off his office and allow the FBI to investigate in a prescribed manner. Instead, the opposite occurred the day Foster died. Some of Clinton's top White House aides, including Patsy Thomasson, Bernie Nussbaum and Maggie Williams, in a dramatic exhibition of bravado, barged into Foster's office and removed all the evidence to Hillary's closet upstairs.

Somehow the FBI and the Park Police sat by for two hours watching while this was going on. Later, an FBI agent filed a complaint for obstruction of justice. Guess what? "Slick Willy" stepped in and had the matter closed. That might come out at the hearings.

Vince Foster was Clinton's counsel for "Whitewater". Yes, he could have killed himself on July 20, 1993, as Robert Fiske, Clinton's "independent" counsel claimed. However, the Fiske story has the following holes in it. As a result, some sources suspect that former Judge Kenneth Starr replaced Fiske for that very reason. Here are some of the problems in Fiske's report:

> - On July 19, 1993, the day before he died, Foster hired two lawyers. He knew that he had failed as Clinton's man in charge of the "Whitewater" cover-up. As a lawyer himself, he could see that everything was coming apart. He wanted to get legal advice because he knew that he would be defending his own position in this cover-up. These two lawyers will claim attorney-client privilege in the hearings, even though their client died the next day. The advice they gave him will never be known. The question is, did that advice cause their client to become despondent and see no other way out, except to end it all by suicide, or was it a set-up and someone else pulled the trigger?

> - Foster was the highest government official to meet an untimely death since Robert Kennedy was shot by Sirhan Sirhan in Los

18

Angeles. Foster was left handed, official photos of the body show the gun was held in his right hand. There were no fingerprints on that gun. Imagine if you are about to kill yourself how nervous you would be. Can you conceive holding the gun and pulling the trigger at a moment like that, with the wrong hand? Then somehow, after you blew your brains out, you wipe off your fingerprints.

- When Foster's body was found, his glasses were thirteen feet away, among bushes. His body was laying perfectly straight, legs together, arms straight down at each side, gun in the right hand, trickles of dried blood running from his mouth in many directions, including uphill. The bullet was never found, even though a massive search and a large excavation, sifted through a fine sieve, was conducted.

- A paramedic and his assistant insisted that Foster's body was first found two hundred feet from the "official spot" where it was later reported. There were no bone fragments from the skull found anywhere. A .38 caliber bullet will usually cause a large hole, three to four inches, as it leaves the head, scattering bone fragments, brain tissue and blood over a wide area. Sophisticated hit men repack their cartridges with a half charge because that's all it takes to kill through the head. It also makes less noise, and, as in Foster's skull, it leaves a smaller

19

hole. A one inch hole was in the back of Foster's skull.

After lunch that day, Vince left the White House, saying "I will be back". It is suspected Vince went to see his girlfriend. It is rumored that he and Hillary were lovers at one time. Blond hairs were found on Vince's clothes. There were carpet fibers on his legs and a trace of semen was found on his shorts.

Vince never came back to the White House as he said he would. The Hearings may show that he went to the girlfriend's apartment, had sex, and then was killed somewhere between that apartment and the place that his body was found. What about a suicide note? The only thing that Vince wrote was an unsigned draft of a letter of resignation. Clinton's counsel, Bernard Nussbaum, kept that letter for a few days after he ransacked Foster's office the afternoon of his death. The FBI had by then inspected Foster's briefcase, found it to be empty. Yet after those few days, a miracle took place. The resignation letter was found in the same briefcase, torn into 27 pieces, no fingerprints on any of them, and the 28th piece, the last one on the page, was missing. This was not a suicide note.

Witnesses may testify at the hearing that a large, rough, South American man was seen at the site where Foster's body was discovered. The man was seen standing next to a white van with the side door open.

Clinton's defense lawyers will say that Foster was cracking up; because of the pressure put on him by his boss, this could have been so. They will say that he killed himself, not true. But let's assume he did. The next question is why?

Was Vince so sensitive to criticism that he just couldn't take it any more? Fiske already stated that those close to Vince said:

> "The single greatest source of his distress was the criticism he received following the firing of seven employees from the White House Travel Office".

The scandal that would impeach his President was not Travelgate, it was "Whitewater"! The thought of being the central figure in an investigation which would lead to the first impeachment in history of the the President of the United States of America could have caused him to pull the trigger. Did it?

According to some sources, the hearings will determine that it did not, and that Clinton has, in all probability, no defense, except perhaps insanity, but of course that is only speculation based on rumor.

The former FBI Director, William Sessions, may be called to testify at the "Whitewater" Hearings. Watch and listen to his testimony carefully. Clinton is the first President ever in the history of the U.S.A. to have fired his FBI Director. This desperate event took place right after Sessions was to subpoena documents from a judge in Arkansas.

As you may remember, this judge charged Clinton with fraudulent SBA loans totaling millions of dollars to Clinton's friends. Vince Foster found out about this intended subpoena on the day he died. His brother-in-law, Beryl Anthony, a former congressman, and Foster's sister should testify on this at the "Whitewater" Hearings.

Dennis Hopper starred in a movie called "Double Crossed". It was about a drug-running operation. Barry Seal's story was portrayed in that movie. Apparently, Barry became a multimillionaire. He was a pilot and supplied planes in what may be alleged was an incredibly elaborate and successful drug-running operation out of Mena, Arkansas.

A top selling book entitled "Compromised" by Terry Reed and John Cummings contains additional information about the apparent money laundering through the Bank of Credit & Commerce International (BBCI) from the Mena, Arkansas operations. It makes you wonder if the U.S. Government is the most powerful drug dealer on earth?

Everyone knew that Iran-Contra was a scheme to use the Ayatollah's money to send guns to the Contra freedom fighters. In the process, Ollie North and Bill Clinton might have discovered each other. Then it sort of somehow became an Arkansas enterprise.

A-K 47's and other arms were sent from Mena, Arkansas to Nicaragua. Return flights called "Black Flights", came back with loads of drugs and cash from Columbia via the Cayman Islands, or Panama. "Black Flights" are special flights that customs officials and air traffic controllers

22

are instructed to ignore.

Testimony from witnesses at the hearings may show that Clinton, as well as Ollie North, were both aware of what was going down in Mena. Bill Plante, CBS news correspondent, and Michael Singer, producer, CBS News, on May 3, 1994 wrote in a letter to the editor of the Wall Street Journal:

> "...Former Clinton Staff people have told CBS News that the Governor was aware of what was going on there.
>
> Mena is a perplexing and difficult story. There is a trail--tens of millions of dollars in cocaine profits, and we don't know where it leads. It is a trail that has been blocked by the National Security Council.
>
> The FAA, FBI, Customs, CIA, Justice, DEA, and the IRS were all involved in Mena. They won't say how they were involved, but they will tell you there is nothing there."

Charles Black, Polk County Prosecutor, asked Clinton himself to conduct a State investigation of Mena. In 1988, Governor Clinton said he would get back to him. Somehow, he never did. An article in Penthouse Magazine related the following:

> "He (Clinton) controlled virtually all the 2,000 handpicked appointees to an array of boards and commissions that effectively rule

23

the state... Anyone seeking to do business with or in the state of Arkansas learned to expect direct solicitations by Clinton's campaign finance people."

A state controlled that tightly is by and of itself a breeding ground for corruption. The hearings will probably bring out testimony that Barry Seal was gunned down by Colombian thugs, as shown in the movie. When that happened, Clinton was reportedly quoted:

"Seal just got too damn big for his britches and that scum had to die, in my opinion."

Eventually, "Slick Willy" and his friends got "too big for their britches" and the Mena operation was quietly moved to Mexico. In the "Whitewater" Hearings you may hear testimony about Reagan's CIA Director, William Casey, being aware of the money laundering and drug-running in Arkansas. What happened to Mr. Casey?---he died, how?

We don't know, but we understand that two Bryant, Arkansas teenagers, Kevin Ives and Don Henry, were found dead on August 23, 1987, run over by a train. State Medical Examiner, Famey Mallock, a Clinton appointee, declared;

"They fell asleep on the tracks."

Sure they did. Like a lot of teenage boys, they put their head on a steel rail and took a nap. It happens everywhere! Trains roll over teenagers almost everyday!

Kevin and Don were observing events at night near Mena. Apparently they were caught and never came home. Joseph Burton, State of Georgia Medical Examiner, performed a second autopsy on each body. He proved that Kevin was struck in the head and Don was stabbed. Their bodies were mutilated by the train so badly that the cause of death remained uncertain. There were six people who claimed to have some knowledge of how the boys died on those tracks. They were;

Keith Coney	Jeff Rhodes
Richard Winters	Keith McKaskle
Gregory Collins	Jordan Ketelson

Before any of the above were able to give testimony, they all died from gun or knife wounds. The hearings may expose how they died and why they died. In all probability, the families of these eight young men will testify.

If all that has been said about Mena leads to Clinton, that evidence is then the most serious set of allegations ever brought against a President of the United States. It would certainly make the "Whitewater" land deal pale in order of importance. If, indeed the CBS News report is true, and the FAA, FBI, Customs, CIA, Justice, Drug Enforcement, and the IRS are all covering up, then the answers to these questions are buried in federal bureaucracy. Each question, unanswered, in an important matter such as "Mena", leads to more questions. For instance: Why did former senator and Clinton's treasury secretary, Lloyd Benson, quit? Why did Senator George Mitchell quit after failing to conduct the "Whitewater" investigation properly the first time around? Etc..., etc....Some say Benson did a lousy job - perhaps he did more.

Danny Casolaro, a reporter investigating the connection between Mena, BCCI, Iran Contra, Park-On Meter Co. and Arkansas Development Finance Authority was found dead in the bathtub of a hotel room in West Virginia, on August 10, 1991.

Paul Wilcher, a Washington, D.C. lawyer, was scheduled to meet with Danny Casolaro's former attorney. He was found dead that day in his apartment on June 22, 1993.

Little is known about why Ed Willey, the manager of Clinton's Presidential Campaign Finance Committee he shot himself on November 30, 1993. There may be an inquiry into that shooting. The hearings may expose that he was, at one time, "shuffling" briefcases full of cash at Mena.

John A. Wilson, city councilman in Washington, D.C., was familiar with Clinton's operations. He was prepared to come forward and tell all, but instead, on May 19, 1993, he just decided to hang himself.

There have been several air crash deaths of former Clinton intimates and advisors. Those numbers defy all known statistics on air travel. It's amazing that all FAA reports on these air traffic fatalities just don't exist. The hearings might show that at least four of them are probably connected with Clinton's scandals.

* C. Victor Riser, II, former Finance Co-Chairman of Clinton's presidential campaign and his son, Monty. On July 30, 1992, in good weather near Anchorage, Alaska, their plane crashed, killing both father and son instantly. Riser was respected as a man of integrity. He may not have liked what he perceived as campaign shenanigans. As a result, he could have become a threat to the presidency of Bill Clinton. Three months before the election. He may have paid for his honesty.

* In a light drizzle, on March 1, 1994, a plane exploded as it approached a private airstrip in Arkansas. The airstrip and plane belonged to Herschel Friday, a member of Riser's committee and a well known gentleman. The pilot and Mr. Friday were aboard.

* Two days later, on March 3, 1994, after Herschel Friday died, Dr. Ronald Rogers, a dentist from Royal, Arkansas, was on his way to a meeting when his twin engined Cessna crashed, with a full tank of fuel, near Lawton, Oklahoma. On board was Reiford Rogers, his brother. The pilot, Russell Boyd, radioed ahead that he was on empty and the engines had stopped. There were no survivors.

The hearings may bring out evidence about a sabotage technique that has been used effectively on small planes, causing crashes such as killed Riser, his son, Rogers and Friday.

More about the Clintons.

Hillary and Bill give undivided attention to details; for instance, their 1979 Income Tax Return reported Bill's used undershorts as a charitable contribution, valued at two dollars a pair. (Who do you suppose did the undershorts appraisal?) That's about as fine as anyone can massage the "poor old" IRS.

However, you may recall how Clinton proclaimed over and over again that he forgot to deduct $68,900 he claims he lost on "Whitewater". That seems like a mystery vis-a-vis the used shorts deduction. In reality, it's no mystery at all. Clinton didn't lose a penny on "Whitewater". He is just smart enough not to get caught and do time for tax fraud. If the hearings verify all of this, maybe he will do time for taxpayer fraud? Isn't that the same offense?

As you can clearly see, what is labeled as "Whitewater" is an umbrella for a lot of other deals masterminded by the J.R. Ewings and the Alexis Carrington Colbys of Arkansas. Some of these characters may end up in jail, even though they are smart enough to shred subpoenaed documents and avoid tax fraud.

There are plenty of people out in Arkansas that are alive and hurt by all of this. They want to get even. Their testimony at the hearings could "sink" the Clintons and others. It's up to us, I don't know about you, but I am "<u>mad as hell</u>" about all of this and I want it cleaned up. <u>Every American taxpayer, and Senator Alfonse M. D'Amato, and Representative Jim Leach, are charged with the responsibility to make sure all the facts are brought out and examined in the open</u>.

The proof of the pudding is that Bill Clinton entered public office with nothing but debt. He only made $35,000 per year as Governor. That's not a part time job. He had no other source of income. Now he is reportedly worth $5,000,000 without counting what may be in overseas secret bank accounts. It is reported that Foster opened a bank accounts in Geneva and Zurich in Chelsea Jefferson's name. The accounts allegedly hold $50,000,000.00. It is a good ol' fashion "American Dream" story "from rags to riches".

Do you know why medical costs have skyrocketed since 1980? The cost of medical care, prescription drugs, hospitalization and out patient treatment has gone up over 1000 percent since then. The answer is that prior to 1980, medicine and taking care of sick people was not part of the type of profiteering common to Wall Street. Before, there was competition in providing health care. As a result of strategic takeovers of non-profit hospitals by mega-conglomerates, all hospitals in America are now for profit, including those formerly run by religious organizations.

There is no competition in medical services now. It's not free enterprise either. Medicine in America is a "cartel" run by the American Medical Association and big business. A cartel is defined as a combination of independent, private enterprises supplying like commodities or services, that agree to limit competitive activities by allocating customers or markets, thus regulating quality and quantity, fixing prices or terms of sale, exchanging techniques, and methods of service, controlling price, promotion and distribution, in a bloc.

In America, it is illegal to control competition through such cartels. It is doubly illegal to pay members of such cartels with our Medicare tax dollars.

If it's not six hundred-forty dollar toilets, purchased by the defense department with our money, as was the case under the Reagan Administration. It's twenty dollars per pill for aspirin at every hospital in America, paid for with our money, by Medicare, under the Clinton Administration.

After graduating from Arkansas real estate deals like "Whitewater", and drug deals in Mena, what could be better for "Slick Willy" and Hillary, than getting in on the action of "The American Medical Cartel"?

Have we ever had a president that's been accused of being involved in just about every illegal activity that exists? What's really important is that every one of these deals costs you and me a lot of money. How many similar deals go down every day in Washington, D.C.? How much out of every one of our tax dollars goes to these deals? Don't you think we should know?

Part III

The "Whitewater" Roots:

Alexis Charles Henri Clevel de Tocqueville, a young French aristocrat came to America to examine Democracy in 1831 and in 1835, wrote "*DEMOCRACY IN AMERICA*". To this day his book remains a basic text in American history and political theory. He said in 1835, "I know of no country, indeed, where the love of money has taken a stronger hold on the affections of men." His astute observation included a prediction of the future competition that would arise between the U.S.A. and Russia.

America lacked a native mythology because the Native Americans were cast into what seems an eternal "bad guy" image. The cowboys and Federal Calvary were the proverbial "good guys". The United States had no Odyssey, no Saint George slaying the dragon, no King or Queen as in England. We rejected the fact that "the King can do no wrong". We paid for that freedom in blood during the American Revolution. Now, over two hundred years later, the tyranny of government is back. It is our absolute duty to get rid of that tyranny. We replaced all that with an American genius for making a lot of money. However, that was a poor substitute for King Arthur and his knights. The Horatio Alger myth of "rags to riches" seemed to satisfy the dream, as well as cover up, a lot of sins.

It was in the 19th Century that the American media first found its myth making machinery, the movies. This medium created a suitable heroic archetype from Wild West stories. The image of the American cowboy was portrayed as a sort of ignoble American knight. His life was shown to be one of reckless individualism, brave in the face of the elements in the wide open spaces, driving cattle across the prairies, staving off the savage attacks of Indians. Then, heroic lawmen chasing bank robbers and dueling with six-guns in the street at high noon became an artificial Iliad which plagues us to this day. The leaders of today's militias are very much part of that heritage. They are the "lawmen" of yesteryear, the rugged individuals that once disappeared. Senator Specter and others in government fear them. They fear all individuals. America should embrace them and thank God for their presence.

The heritage of that Iliad lacks nobility, chivalry and a code of ethics, as compared to King Arthur's Camelot. The famed cow and mining towns of Tombstone, Abilene, Dodge City and Deadwood somehow lacked a sense of honor found in the mythological quest for the Holy Grail. By the turn of the century, the Wild West faded out of existence and was replaced by a much more sinister and ornery character, The American Businessman. From the robbers of banks and trains, like Jesse James, our Iliad turned to the Robber Barons of the Industrial Revolution, the J.P. Morgans, the Rockefellers, the Vanderbilts, the Goulds and the Carnegies. In time, these names became symbols of American wealth, aristocracy and nobility. They were epitomized in everyone's living room by the J.R. Ewings and Alexis Colby Carringtons of the 1980's. In the movies, Dirty Harry and other corrupt character, and killers, were taken on as a very lucrative life's work by actors like Clint Eastwood. These killers and bandits are our children's heroes and heroines. Somehow it's quite possible that "monkey see - monkey do" might apply to our juvenile crime problem.

Technically, "Whitewater's" roots go back to the "Great Depression", which was caused by greed. America has had recessions since and depressions before 1928, but none of these had been capitalized like the "Great Depression". As with "Whitewater" the 1928 Depression touched every American and most people throughout the world. To better understand what we are up against in the deluge of "Whitewater", we have to look back in history.

It's difficult, very difficult indeed, to look back at the icons of this century. It is difficult to criticize our "aristocracy". To some, J.F.K. meant so much hope that if he is criticized, it enrages those who thought fondly of him. Unfortunately, there is a price that must be paid for the clarity of events past. Commercial packaging of Presidents by those who profit from it, at our expense, was the mist we could not see through. Some will get violently angry as those commercial bubbles burst. Some of the events which brought us to this terrible calamity are illustrated as background information to clarify an objective non-partisan view of "Whitewater".

After the 1929 "Crash", 1,300 banks failed. Federal Deposit Insurance did not exist. The hard earned savings of working people disappeared when 5,000 more banks closed during the next three years. These banks had their assets tied up in credit on speculations that created the wealth, which seemed to disappear overnight with the "Crash" on Black Thursday.

It was a vicious circle. Jobs were lost, mortgages were defaulted by the unemployed, as a result, banks went under, thereby causing a giant credit crunch. There was no capital to finance business, factories, or all the other types of commercial establishments. Businesses closed their doors forcing more unemployment. The misery this broken system caused the American people, devastated the nation.

It's important to note that before the Great Depression, Americans were able to absorb periodic depressions as a much less devastating experience. It was simply because most people lived on farms and were able to produce what they needed. Before the industrialization and resulting urbanization of America, the "rugged individual" was the strength of this great nation.

When those "rugged individuals" gave up their independence of fending for themselves and moved to the cities, then they became dependent on a job. Employment provided the means to own a home, which depended on financing. The services necessary to live a life in a city depended on government, and it depended on taxes. In a few decades, that "rugged individual" that made America great became totally dependent on others, and thereby lost that individuality. This was magnified to horrible proportions by an event like the "Great Depression". Some historians claim that 40 - 50 percent of all jobs in America were lost. Homelessness was rampant. In those days, people who lost their homes were called "Hobos". This term was applied to hundreds of thousands of wandering men, women and children who roamed the country in search of food, shelter and jobs.

The "Establishment" in those days consisted of men like Henry Ford, who put 75,000 men out of work in one day. Later he said, "It's the best education in the world for those boys, that traveling around!"

Andrew Mellon, the founder of the Mellon Bank of Pittsburg, said, "Liquidate labor, liquidate stocks, liquidate the farmer, liquidate real estate, people will work harder, live a more moral life, values will be adjusted and enterprising people will pick up the wrecks from less competent people."

Herbert Hoover, the President, had a similar attitude. He refused to allow government to issue direct aid. According to him, it was socialism to do so, and was completely contrary to his notion of "rugged individualism". As a result, there were no government programs to help the jobless, homeless or starving Americans.

No one in the U.S. Government wanted to be called a Socialist or a Communist for even suggesting such relief - in spite of the growing misery of "Hoovervilles", communities of cardboard shacks, thrown up in all of America's large cities, caused the deepening despair of hundreds of thousands without hope. Nothing was done, until Roosevelt seized this pitiful condition as a political opportunity, and got himself elected President. What really clinched the election for Roosevelt was the "Bonus Army".

In the summer of 1932, an election year, the Depression reached its peak. Nearly 100,000 World War I veterans walked, hitchhiked or "rode the rails" with their families to Washington, D.C. in protest. This "Bonus Expeditionary Force", (BEF) as they called themselves, was a penniless, vagrant army.

They took over abandoned buildings along Pennsylvania Avenue and erected a "shanty town" along the Anacostia River. They came to ask Hoover to pay them the bonus promised veterans in 1924. Starving, desperate men, whose families were going hungry. No jobs and no prospects of anything else but continued misery, they wanted and needed that bonus. Later they were known as the "Bonus Army".

To the "Establishment", Congress, Hoover, lawmen, and newspapers (media), they weren't veterans, but Communist Agitators - even though the Veterans Administration verified that 95 percent of the "Bonus Army" were veterans. Instead of meeting their leaders, Hoover called out the troops. Amazing as it may seem, the commander was General Douglas MacArthur, and his aide was Dwight Eisenhower. The attack on their fellow Americans was lead by the Third Calvary, sabers ready, commanded by none other than Major George S. Patton.

Patton's Calvary first charged this ragged bunch of men, women and children and cut them down. Then came the tear gas, tanks and foot soldiers with bayonets. The "Bonus Army" retreated over the Eleventh Street Bridge, across the river. General MacArthur, true to form as he became famous for throughout his career, decided to finish them off.

After nightfall, the tanks leveled that shanty town and what was left was torched. As a result, over 132 American

Veterans, 12 women and 2 children were killed by their own government, because they were starving and wanted to claim the bonus promised them. Instead of paying them what was owed, their own government killed them, and the rest staggered off somewhere. There was no home for them, except oblivion.

Roosevelt promised a "New Deal", and after his inauguration, the "Bonus Army" got a "New Deal". The veterans returned to Washington, D.C. Roosevelt asked Eleanor to go and speak to the men, women and children. She did more than that; she fed them and gave them hot coffee. The first lady mingled with the group and led them in song.

It was said in the press, "Hoover sent the Army, Roosevelt sent his wife." A remarkable woman and her husband appeared as "angels of mercy", at the right place, at the right time. What they did was correct, compassionate and just. No one will ever argue with that statement. They took care of Americans with American taxpayers money, as it should be.

A few days after F.D.R. took residence in the White House, he started his "fireside chats" - radio addresses aimed at educating the public, soothing fears, and restoring the confidence and optimism of a nation near bankruptcy. Then he called a special emergency session of congress to meet for 100 days. That phrase, "The First One Hundred Days", we have heard so much about from Newt Gingrich, was born 62 years ago. The U.S. Congress came together and F.D.R. pushed through extraordinary legislation. It was done so fast that most congressmen and senators passed it without even reading the content.

Roosevelt's approach was "Take a method and try it. If it fails, try another". Remember, that this was a last ditch approach at saving the nation from ruin caused by the greed of its citizens and big business. It was absolutely necessary to do what was done, but when the nation got back on its feet, those programs lingered, and grew in some instances into huge bureaucracies which should have been dismantled as soon as they served their purpose. The fact that F.D.R. was re-elected to four terms in office speaks for itself. No politician after that example dared to reduce Federal spending. Now we are forced to.

The "New Deal" was a turning point in American history, as decisive as the Revolution of 1776 or the Civil War of 1860. It transformed the federal government from a small, insignificant presence in the lives of Americans, to a huge bureaucracy that left few Americans untouched. F.D.R. injected federal government into American veins with unprecedented doses.

Today in 1995, it has become a total addiction. Previously, this was an unthinkable reliance on government to solve the problems of a private economy. The machinery of government created to carry the nation out of one crisis overstayed its welcome, thus creating other crises in its wake.

Ever since then, liberal democrats were considered saviors of our country, while staunch conservatives, who tried to stop the tide of giveaways, were ridiculed as the enemy. In hindsight, we have to acknowledge that since then, we the voters, the owners of America, were not "minding the store". "Whitewater" is a direct result of that indifference.

When Harry Truman is considered in the context of "Whitewater", we have to acknowledge that his contribution to its roots was mostly in what is known as the "Truman Doctrine". The Truman Doctrine, for the first time in history, extended the federal government's peace-time influence beyond our borders. Roosevelt's "Lend-Lease" was a sort of footstool to what happened after President Truman told Congress;

> "I believe that it must be the policy of the United States to support free peoples who are resisting subjugation by armed minorities or by outside pressure."

The ensuing foreign policy of "Containment" is still with us and has been applied by Clinton in Haiti as recently as a few months ago. After World War II ended, America was in no financial position to give foreign aid or assistance to anyone. The "Truman Doctrine" propelled us into preventing a Communist takeover of Greece and Turkey; that's how it was sold.

The disease was Communism, led by Joseph Stalin in the U.S.S.R. He got away with half of Europe when it was handed to him by Roosevelt and Churchill at Yalta. That was an inexcusable mistake. Historians have not yet fully explained the severity of what happened at that time. It has been ruinous to the world since, and the price Americans and others have had to pay for that blunder can never be calculated. Suffice it to say, General George S. Patton could have crushed the Soviet Union Army at the end of World War II as he crushed the "Bonus Army" in 1932.

Everyone knew who the real enemy was at the end of WWII. Instead of terminating Stalin, we promoted Communism by allowing him to enslave solid, good people who helped us beat the Nazis. Over 200 million citizens of Poland, Czechoslovakia, Hungary, Yugoslavia, Romania, Bulgaria, Latvia, Estonia, Lithuania, Germany and Albania became slaves of Joseph Stalin, and thereby expanded Communism by nearly doubling its base, in terms of potential party members.

The Truman Doctrine was nothing more than a band-aid applied to a severe head wound hemorrhaging away the blood of politically expedient people left to rot for fifty years. Lech Walesa of Poland, started and accomplished the overthrow of Communism with a peaceful revolution, which did not cost us a penny.

For that effort, vis-a-vis, the trillions of dollars that our Democrat and Republican Presidents spent on so called "defense against the spread of Communism", Walesa should be named the "Man of the Century". We should question the wisdom of those defense efforts and the veracity of those horrendous budgets. That track record, and its hidden agenda, as compared to Mr. Walesa's has to be scrutinized very carefully by historians in the future.

It is interesting to note that in 1947, the Twenty-Second Amendment to the U.S. Constitution was ratified limiting a president to two terms or to a single elected term for a president who has served more than two years of his predecessor's term, as Truman had. Consider the fact that term limits were then imposed on the presidency because of F.D.R.'s four consecutive terms and a fear of the possibility of ensuing American dictatorships.

It is clear that today, in 1995, we have been strangled by a sort of congressional dictatorship by the two party system, which prides itself on what ought to be the most feared euphemism in American history, "Business as usual". When you hear those words, realize what they mean. To spell it out so it's absolutely clear, they mean:

"We got you again sucker and we will make you pay through the nose!"

(signed)

Republicans & Democrats

In 1952, Eisenhower and Nixon were elected. Eisenhower was brought in to fight and win the Korean War, which started under the "Truman Doctrine" in 1950. The cost was more than 150,000 American lives, 2 million Korean lives, and several billion dollars of American taxpayers money. The result, a half-baked partition, which accomplished nothing, and is still with us to this day.

The most significant contribution Eisenhower's Presidency made to the beginnings of "Whitewater" was the preoccupation of his administration with running the Cold War in a vacuum of moral leadership at home. The "Cold War-General" was making money for the Industrial Military Complex under his vision of making "the world safe for Democracy". However, that vision had a myopic periphery when it came to Black Americans and U.S. education as a whole.

41

Fortunately for us, in those days, the system of checks and balances between the executive, legislative and judicial branches of government still worked. Eisenhower appointed Earl Warren as Chief Justice of the Supreme Court. Thank God for Chief Justice Warren. He was a very fair and intelligent man.

Brown vs. Board of Education, May 17, 1954: that decision was orchestrated by Warren and he shaped the consensus of the court to overthrow what was legal, separating black children from white children in public schools. That simple, unanimous opinion, without dissent, was one of the most significant contributions to our democracy ever made. It read;

> "We come then to the question presented: Does segregation of children in public schools solely on basis of race, even though the physical facilities and other 'tangible' factors may be equal, deprive the children of the minority group of equal education opportunities? We believe that it does....
>
> To separate them from others of similar age and qualifications solely because of their race generates a feeling of inferiority as to their status in the community that may affect their hearts and minds in a way unlikely ever to be undone....
>
> ...We conclude that in the field of public education the doctrine of 'separate but equal' has no place. Separate educational facilities are inherently unequal."

This historic judgment gave the civil rights movement the green light. In that context, Martin Luther King, Jr. began to lead, what was to be, an illustrious march out of bondage, for Americans who happened to have a dark color to their skin.

Throughout this important time, Eisenhower stood in a vacuum of moral leadership on civil rights issues. The Republican Party was incapable of accepting the court's decision gracefully. In defiance of the law of the land, in September 1957, the former Governor of Arkansas, Orville Faubus, posted the Arkansas National Guard outside Little Rock Central High School. Their orders were to prevent nine black children from entering the all white school. People from all over the world watched as the children tried to enter the school, but were turned away. The fully armed guardsmen and a jeering mob, spat on and cursed those nine innocent children. The media exposed this incident to millions of viewers on television, worldwide.

Eisenhower did nothing. He was apparently fearful of alienating the powerful bloc of "Dixiecrats", southern democratic congressmen, whose votes he needed and who did not want integration. Finally, after the media exposé, Eisenhower gave the order to send in federal troops to Little Rock to quell the riots and enforce the law of the land. The troops remained in Little Rock Central High School for the rest of the school year.

The racial hatred toward "Negroes" in the South was glorified in what came to be known as "The Southern Manifesto", authored by ninety-six U.S. congressmen, in response to the Supreme Court's decision.

...This unwarranted exercise of power by the court, contrary to the Constitution, is creating chaos and confusion in the states principally affected. It is destroying the *amicable relations between the white and Negro races that have been created through ninety years of patient effort by good people of both races.* (Emphasis added.) It has planted hatred and suspicion where there has been heretofore friendship and under standing.

In his farewell address, given on January 17, 1961, Eisenhower sounded a bit like an animal trainer who let the lion out of the cage, yelling "look out!" A leading proponent of Cold War "Containment" and an advocate of the "Truman Doctrine", Eisenhower presided over the birth and adolescence of the "Military-Industrial Complex". Yet he said the following:

"The conjunction of an immense military establishment and large arms industry is new in the American experience. The total influence-economic, political, even spiritual- -is felt in every city, every state house, every office of the federal government. We recognize the imperative need for the development. Yet we must not fail to comprehend its grave implications. Our toil, resources, and livelihood are all involved; so is the very structure of our society.

In the councils of government, we must guard against the acquisitions of unwarranted influence, whether sought or unsought, by the military-industrial complex. The potential for the disastrous rise of misplaced power exists and will persist."

This speech is a sort of "bad guy-good guy", two party system doctrine used by Democrats to blame Republicans, and vice-versa, to keep the grease flowing and to perpetuate "Business as usual". "Whitewater" is directly descended from that gamesmanship.

The Age of Aquarius gave us "all you need is love". Jack Kennedy, and his post-mortem by Jackie, "Camelot". In the meantime, while he was alive, J.F.K., during sexual time outs, tried to run the country. His father, Joe Kennedy, Henry Luce, William Randolph Hearst, Frank Sinatra and Mafia mobsters all helped our first Catholic president into office. Unfortunately, Sinatra introduced J.F.K. to Judith Campbell (Exner), who became a regular Kennedy sex partner in "Camelot". Sinatra forgot to tell Jack, or his brother Robert, that Judith was also sleeping at the same time with Sam Giancana, the Mafia chief, and his hit man, John Roselli. The result of that little quadrangle was a contract given to Roselli to pull off the CIA planned assassination of Fidel Castro. Roselli got paid, but Castro is still here.

You can't blame J.F.K. After all, he gave us the Bay of Pigs, the Cuban Missile Crisis, the Peace Corps and Women's Liberation. J.F.K was the best commercial

President ever. Even though he cheated on his wife, he and she were sold to the naive America voters as the beginning of a dynasty which was to give us a superior identity. We all cheered the prospect of a royalty of sorts and a tradition that was missing from the beginning. We bought it "hook, line & sinker". It felt so good to swallow that potion because we needed it. We still do. We are in a constant, weary search for credibility; as King Arthur's knights looked for the "Holy Grail", we look for credibility.

One of the great events of Kennedy's epoch was not manufactured by him. It was real, not phony, and not "Establishment" made. History will remember the following speech given in Washington D.C. in August of 1963, longer than anything J.F.K. ever said or did:

> "I say to you today, my friends, that in spite of the difficulties and frustrations of the moment I still have a dream. It is a dream deeply rooted in the American dream.
>
> I have a dream that one day this nation will rise up and live out the true meaning of its creed: 'We hold these truths to be self-evident; that all men are created equal.'
>
> I have a dream that one day on the red hills of Georgia the sons of former slaves and the sons of former slave owners will be able to sit down together at the same table of brotherhood.

I have a dream that one day even the state of Mississippi, a desert state sweltering with the heat of injustice and oppression, will be transformed into an oasis of freedom and justice.

I have a dream that my four children will one day live in a nation where they will not be judged by the color of their skin but by the content of their character.

I have a dream today.

I have a dream that one day the state of Alabama, whose governor's lips are presently dripping with the words of interposition and nullification, will be transformed into a situation where little black boys and black girls will be able to join hands with little white boys and white girls and walk together as sisters and brothers.

I have a dream today...."

Rev. Martin Luther King, Jr.

Most Americans to this day are not satisfied with the answer to the question: Who was the boss behind the triggers that killed Jack and Robert Kennedy? We will never know the answer. Let us not lapse into the same dumbfounded stupor of awe when Bill Clinton's deeds are examined during the "Whitewater" hearings. "Hear no evil, speak no evil and see no evil" has to be reversed in "Whitewater" to; "Let's expose the evil, hear it, see it, talk about it and face it, so that we can eliminate it.

Lyndon Baines Johnson gave a great speech during his campaign of 1964 and trounced Barry Goldwater:

> "The Great Society rests on abundance and liberty for all. It demands an end to poverty and racial injustice, to which we are totally committed in our time. But that is just the beginning.
>
> The Great Society is a place where every child can find knowledge to enrich his mind and to enlarge his talents. It is a place where leisure is a welcome chance to build and reflect, not a feared cause of boredom and restlessness. It is a place where the city of man serves not only the needs of the body and the demands of commerce, but the desire for beauty and the hunger for community.
>
> It is a place where man can renew contact with nature. It is a place which honors creation for its own sake and for what it adds to the understanding of the race. It is a place where men are more concerned with the quality of their goals than the quantity of their goods."

L.B.J.'s legislative record was impressive. It contained attacks on racial injustice through economic and educational reforms and programs aimed at ending the cycle of poverty. The Civil Rights Bill proposed by Kennedy was passed and L.B.J. signed it into law. The Office of Economic Opportunity was created. The Voting Rights Act, the Job Corps, the Head Start Program, Medicaid and Medicare were all passed during Johnson's term. It was the most ambitious social revolution since F.D.R.'s New Deal. Unfortunately for L.B.J.'s legacy, he and his cronies led us down the primrose path of the Vietnam War. His place in history will be marked oddly enough not for what he accomplished, but for what he couldn't change.

The Vietnam War started for Americans in 1950 when Truman guaranteed military aid to France, in accordance with the "Truman Doctrine". Ultimately, the American taxpayer paid over 80 percent of France's military cost against Ho Chi Minh and his Communist rebels in Indochina.

In 1954, Eisenhower considered the use of thermonuclear bombs, but at the last minute decided not to Nuke the Vietnamese people. Instead, he continued to give American tax dollars to the French. The French, with all of that money you and I paid them, lost the war anyway. In May of 1954, Dienbienphu was overrun by Vietnamese rebels. The French withdrew from Indochina and guess what, U.S. foreign policy once again concluded to partition a sovereign country, Vietnam, north and south.

Then, after spending several hundred million dollars helping the anti-communist Saigon government of Ngo-Dink Diem, the Republic of Vietnam was proclaimed. As a result of a rigged election organized by the CIA. Diem, was placed as "the people's choice", and made Prime Minister. In 1959 we started sending troops. That lasted until April 29, 1975, when the last Americans known to be in Vietnam, were evacuated in defeat from Saigon. Approximately 58,000 Americans died for, as Robert McNamara recently pointed out, "a mistake". History will mark Johnson, not Kennedy, responsible.

In June of 1971, a headline appeared in the New York Times: "Pentagon Study Traces Three Decades of U.S. Involvement in Indochina". The "Pentagon Papers" were printed. When the story broke, Americans learned how they had been duped by their own government. Thirty years of deceit and ineptitude were exposed all the way back to Truman. The revelations in the "Pentagon Papers" fueled antiwar sentiment from the college and university campuses to the the halls of Congress.

What happened then may happen now when this book is released. The Nixon administration tried to bully the Times into halting publication. Attorney General John Mitchell threatened the paper with espionage charges. Then Nixon went to federal court, obtained a temporary injunction blocking further publication. It was too late; the Washington Post and the Boston Globe were now running the documents. Again, Nixon tried to stop the truth from coming out. He stopped the Post by court order. On June 30, 1971, the U.S. Supreme Court came through. On a six to three vote, it ruled for the newspapers on the First Amendment grounds.

Kissinger and Nixon went ballistic. "I want to know who is behind this... I want it stopped, whatever the cost!!!" Then Kissinger and Nixon decided to stop the leaks, so they brought in the "plumbers", ex-FBI agent G. Gordon Liddy and former CIA man, E. Howard Hunt. They broke into Daniel Ellsberg's psychiatrists office; then they followed with another break-in, at an office complex called Watergate.

From the Oval Office, tapes of Richard Nixon's voice said:

> "I don't give a shit what happens, I want you to stonewall it. Let them plead the Fifth Amendment, cover-up, or anything else, if it'll save the plan."

The roots of "Whitewater" are easily seen in Watergate, which was an overt example of a "Bunker mentality" developed in the minds of the "Palace Guard" at the White House. The "us against them" defensiveness, which emanated from the Oval Office in the Nixon days, already discovered itself last year during that feeble attempt known as the first "Whitewater" hearings. In all probability, it will continue to come out in lies and more lies, until the truth is out in the open. If he is found guilty, Clinton ought not to be pardoned by his successor, as Nixon was pardoned by Gerald Ford. However, if he is pardoned by the next president, that will be the foundation used and Gerald Ford will go down in history as the precedent setting president who was responsible for letting two crooks off the hook. Shamefully, they will have been presidents of the United States of America.

Watergate, the revelations of the Pentagon Papers and Gerald Ford's pardon of Nixon, cost the Republicans the

White House in 1976. It was assumed that abuses of that kind were now under control and that White House staff would not undertake such illegal action.

Jimmy Carter, a nice guy from a peanut farm, pledged to rid Washington D.C. of its corruption and became President. Unfortunately for him, international events in the Middle East, dashed Carter's hope of governing effectively. The oil crisis of the prior years and the overthrow of the Shah of Iran were major factors. The Shah was a military dictator installed in 1954 through a CIA backed coup.

Carter's claim to fame in the annals of history will be the Peace Treaty between Egypt and Israel in 1978. However, his demise came from the assault on the American Embassy in Teheran by only five hundred Iranians. The ensuing hostage crisis, Carter's inability to free those Americans, the failed attempt at rescue, which left eight Americans dead in Iran, ended disastrously. It was a classic example of a weak, nice man, who was totally over his head in an international crisis. He has been trying to make up for it ever since. Bill Clinton has exhibited similar tendencies in his vacillating proposals on the Bosnia Crisis and just about everything else in his administration. Carters contributions to the roots of "Whitewater" are insignificant, as was his term in office. However, he did prophetically speak on July 15, 1979 about the forthcoming crisis which is now here.

> "All the legislation in the world can't fix what's wrong with America. So I want to speak with you first tonight about a subject even more serious than energy or inflation.

I want to talk to you right now about a fundamental threat to American Democracy....

The threat is nearly invisible in ordinary ways. It is a crisis of confidence. It is a crisis that strikes at the very heart and soul and spirit of our national will. We can see this crisis in the growing doubt about the meaning of our own lives and in the loss of a unity of purpose for our Nation.

The erosion of our confidence in the future is threatening to destroy the social and political fabric of America."

Ronald Reagan, the cowboy actor, a resurrected celluloid hero, rode into the White House as if he were singing "Happy Trails, to you". We understood him so clearly that we nicknamed him "The Great Communicator". Reagan, however, was handed a script by his makers, the so called "Kitchen Cabinet". The script was performed according to the plot. Reagan gave an Academy Award performance in a play that mesmerized the world for an eight year run; unfortunately it wasn't on Broadway, but on Pennsylvania Avenue, where the stakes are higher, and where we subsidize the cost of production.

There was a simple plot: the gang members of the "Kitchen Cabinet" get richer, as we, the American taxpayers, get poorer. One example of how well this worked was the S&L scandal and the Junk Bond debacle. In the name of "Laissez-Faire Capitalism", Reagan was

53

told to relax "Regulatory Restrictions". He did, for the sole benefit of his advisors selfish interests. Sure some got caught - Michael Milken, Ivan Boesky, Charles Keating - but most got away with our money. The largest deficit in the history of this country was piled up in that eight year run. Have you asked, where did those trillion's of dollars go?

History will one day describe the Reagan Administration as the most corrupt in American history. Another member of Reagan's gang ruined justice in the U.S.A. for generations to come. He was William French Smith, a lawyer, head of a law firm in Los Angeles, Gibson Dunn & Crutcher. Smith became U.S. Attorney General and recommended the appointment of federal judges to his boss. Reagan appointed, for a life term, more than 50 percent of all federal judges during those eight years.

Smith, Ron Gother his successor, and their partners at the firm, got the credit and got very rich in the process. Here is just one example of what followed: As a result, when such a firm's lawyer goes up against an adversary in federal court, and the judge is a Reagan appointee, guess who wins? Right or wrong, law or no law, breach or no breach, Gibson, Dunn & Crutcher wins, always. That law firm's lawyers are permitted to skew, pervert and corrupt justice, and so do the judges. In a case which will be tried in superior court in Los Angeles perhaps this year, that law firm apparently got together with the adversary law firm. They managed to convince the adversary law firm to "take a fall", like the proverbial boxer in a fixed fight. As a result, their client, got away with stealing a four hundred million dollar real estate project called "Montevideo".

The judge who presided over that rip-off said to representatives of both firms, on the record, words to this effect: "Our plan to destroy your client's adversary was very effective." What he was talking about was a totally illegal taking of extremely valuable property without due process. Knowingly, he presided over such a proceeding and then gloated about how proud he was to break the law.

Now, these lawyers are defendants facing what could be a four hundred million dollar malpractice law suit. Suffice it to say, that since 1980, Gibson, Dunn & Crutcher has catapulted into not only national, but international prominence as one of the most powerful firms in America, not because of talent, but because of their undue influence over the justice system. Some will say, so what? Those are the spoils of war. When you win an election you have a right to appoint judges. So you put in some of your friends who take care of you. Wrong! That is what J.R. Ewing does on television, and Clinton emulates in real life. That is what seems to have taken precedence over the U.S. Constitution, and that is what "Whitewater" is all about.

The situation described is a perfect example of how the lawyers, the judges, and the rich, (the "Establishment"), get richer at our expense. A president should not be allowed to ever again do what Reagan did to the Justice System.

Later we had Bush, the understudy, who kept plunging us deeper and deeper into debt. He justified the Defense Department and the "Military Industrial Establishment" "rip-offs" with an economic tonic called "The Kuwait War". He and his advisors believed that if an economic recession is coming, the sure cure is to start a war somewhere.

Now we have Bill and Hillary who tried but failed to pull off the medical scandal of the century. They succeeded with Janet Reno in the Waco Texas Massacre, its roots being in "Whitewater" and Mena. That brief history of events in our lifetime is very difficult to swallow. But it is all the evidence we need to be totally convinced that we cannot trust todays federal government. It's been breaking down and it needs to be rebuilt. We the owners have not been doing our job. We admitted that fact. In a recent poll 76% of Americans say they cannot trust todays federal government. As the saying goes, "deferred maintenance makes the odor unacceptable". Government stinks of corruption.

You can decide for yourself what history has taught us about elected officials. Perhaps they, on the other hand, ought to be made aware that the American people always consistently turn away presidents who are a fraud or who do not serve the interests of the average American.

Hoover was beaten by Roosevelt. Roosevelt promised help and delivered what all Americans needed. Truman did what he had to, and ended World War II for his own people's benefit. Eisenhower built up our defense systems to protect democracy as is known in America. Kennedy was a patented, commercial invention. Johnson had a great vision and started some good programs, but greed in Vietnam sent him into oblivion. Nixon was a crook and got caught at it. Ford, pardoned Nixon. Carter tried to do the right thing, but didn't know how to protect his people, so we sent him packing. Reagan put on a brilliant performance and gave away the equity of this country to his friends. Bush did little else, but he got lucky, on his watch, Communism fell apart. Clinton thought he could run the U.S.A. like he ran the state of Arkansas, and we.......? We who are in charge---What did we do? That chapter has yet to be written.

It's important to remember that we have just reviewed our history for the last seventy years. It is a quick summary of events, most of which are not considered kosher in a democracy. Unfortunately, that has been our track record. Yet we survived all of these scandals and will undoubtedly tolerate more in the future. Someone asked me once, how do I pick my employees? I answered, very carefully---We should pick our next president and vice president the same way. Very Carefully! There is a sideshow going on in California right now with Willie Brown, the recently deposed and much admired, as well as much hated, Speaker of the Assembly. Some say he ruined California's business climate and is now trying to be mayor of San Francisco. Voters in that city ought to examine his deeds very carefully, especially his extra curricular activities, so they know what and whom they are voting for.

Part IV

The Crisis in America:

Sorry to tell you this, but yes, there is a crisis in America. We all know about it and most of us are afraid to face it. It's a credibility crisis. No one can be trusted anymore. Not the president, his first lady and on down. We have this disease, I call it the "Dallas Virus". It's bug is greed. It feeds only on what it can get away with. There is no apparent cure that anyone wants to administer. It's spreading over the entire world and over all generations.

Our federal, state, county and city governments are no exception! Local government corruption is in the news constantly. There is no need for additional comment. The incidents cited from Clinton's history in Arkansas are typical everywhere. Look at Willy Brown, in California. The system starts with the local school board and corrupts all the way to the White House.

The post Oklahoma City bomb "media exposé" of America's militia groups should be of no surprise to most of us who are in tune with the pulse of this Country. Apparently the "Establishment" was caught off guard and it is surprised by the fervor of the Americans involved. The "Establishment" media has it's head in the ground like an ostrich but is quick to blame decent American taxpayers collectively for the Oklahoma City bombing. That is corrupt in and of itself. Our President, the subject of this book said:

"Loud and angry voices in America today... spread hate; they leave the impression by their words, that violence is acceptable."

How can he, accused of so much, say that?

It's very unfortunate that some Americans, in their frustration, resorted to the horror of Oklahoma City. History will hold that the true tragedy of Oklahoma City is corrupt U.S. Government, and unless it changes its "modus operandi" (M.O.), it will kill Democracy and Capitalism as we know it. As Communism died, our system is failing. In both systems, the "Establishment" became too greedy, stopped serving its people, and became totally self-serving. The U.S.S.R. went broke covering up the ruling class's corruption, incompetence and excessive spending on the arms race with America. The U.S.A. is engaged in similar shenanigans.

The 1994 election gathered some hope and inspiration, unfortunately, it took less than "The First Hundred Days" to pierce through the "Contract with America" and to expose it for what it really is. Newt Gingrich decided to sell us down the river. He is a sort of modern day Robespierre. We were set up so he could make millions on his books. We the people of America are apparently not considered Americans in that contract. The "Contract with America" to Newt and the new Republican majority means another deal with special interest groups, not the voters. The "Establishment" is America to Newt. We the taxpayers, the customers, the wage earners, the small business owners, the students, the retired persons, are all lumped as faceless consumers, to be sold another very expensive, but worthless "bill of goods".

Somehow, we are no longer to be considered taxpayers who own America and pay for its government. We are no longer "the customer, who is always right". We are not the hardworking, self respecting, American wage earner. Rather, we are pushed to buy inferior products designed by elite corporate managers, to produce a larger profit for the "Establishment". Somehow, we are not the "Main Street" small business owners who once were the backbone of the economy. We were displaced by politically expedient super warehouses of goods and services built in malls, some of which are owned by foreigners. Somehow, we are no longer the school age Americans who once were the best educated students in the world. Now we are at the bottom, relegated to Third World status in education because of a corrupt federal bureaucracy. Somehow, we are not the respected senior citizens who have retired after a lifetime of hard work and savings. Now those dollars buy less and less because our presidents have decided they have a higher duty to foreign governments, giving away the value of those savings. The dollar is in a free fall. Soon they will sell our Social Security system down the river as well.

We can go on and on about how we are perceived, used and abused by our government and the Establishment. The fact is, they do not think much of us. Because we don't think much of ourselves. It's our fault. As the old saying goes, "Use it or lose it." Our democracy, as we know it, just doesn't work anymore. Why? Could it be that we just didn't pay enough attention to our gift? Could it be that we just didn't participate enough? The government can investigate "Whitewater", Blackwater, Redwater, and whatever bilge water comes up tomorrow, so what? It's irrelevant because, it's fraught with conflicts of interest.

That utopian ideal which was America "for the people and by the people" is no longer. The last item on our Government's agenda is us. We don't have a voice anymore, we lost our voice. We don't vote and we don't participate. Why should they care about our needs?

The "Whitewater" Hearings will go on, they have to. We will sit for weeks in front of the T.V. watching our democracy on trial. It was bound to happen. Clinton just happened to be the wrong guy, in the wrong place, at the wrong time, and we couldn't see through his fabricated image. More than likely he will make a deal, resign, or be pardoned. That's our corrupt system. It was designed for checks and balances; they don't work anymore. The "Establishment" controls the executive, the legislative and the judicial branches of our government. Nothing is checked; the balance tilts heavily towards the "Establishment". It will continue to do so until the average American stops being impressed with "famous people". That alone, an obsession with celebrities, is responsible to a large extent, for the inequities in our democracy. The Clint Eastwoods, the Marilyn Monroes, the Jack Kennedys, the Michael Jordans, the O.J. Simpsons, etc..., and their excessive fame and wealth, corrupt power away from the average person. As a result, all forms of equality in a democracy cease to exist.

The regular media, the "Establishment" controlled news-papers, magazines, television and radio stations, will all get together in their "mutual admiration society" conference rooms across the country and hire some P.R. consultant to put a "spin" on the events to save their behinds. The "spin" will blame parts of the system and it will put off the remedy. That is the expedient thing to do.

They will try to keep the dying corpse of democracy alive by applying some sort of Hollywood make-up. They might even call in the Dream Works of Spielberg, Katzenberg and Geffen to repackage "Whitewater" into a pleasant dream for the consumer, even though it's a total nightmare. Some politician will say "Those boys can do it. They're re-e-e-al go-o-o-o-d." Are you going to buy it?--That's the question!

Remember, what happened in the U.S.S.R. can happen in the U.S.A. The Russians were slaves to their dictatorial form of government and could do nothing. One day they found themselves broke. That will happen in the U.S.A., and it will literally happen tomorrow. Unless we take charge and fix what's wrong today. That's how urgent this crisis is! Ross Perot says he might have the answer. We know he's got some money, that's for sure! Is he another overpaid phenomenon of our system? Or is he a true patriot who really loves this Country and cares about its people? Less than 20 percent of eligible American voters voted Clinton into office. Isn't that amazing? Four out of every five Americans didn't vote for him. We deserve what we got. Now! All of us have to work hard to change all this nonsense.

The militias are ready--do you want them to do it for you?

Part V

Your Participation Is Mandatory:

Unless you say "Enough!!", and participate it's over. Don't let that happen. Don't let extremists take charge. Just stop allowing yourself to be abused by your government. First of all, get informed, seek knowledge even more deliberately than you seek dollars. Then, write to Senator D'Amato and Representative Leach, demand full disclosure on "Whitewater" and send Pebble Beach Press, Ltd. a copy. That way your letters won't get misplaced. We will make sure they get your message. If you wish, you can simply use the pages in the back of this book. Fill in your name, address and telephone number, and send it to us. We will forward it. We provided that for your convenience. Keep your copy and frame it as evidence that you took part in **"The Arkansas Clean Up"**. Tell everyone you know, about this book, ask them to buy one so they can participate, as you are doing. We must have accountability to return common sense to our Country's government. The only way that will happen is if you participate, and **above all** , **vote next time** !

Most of us who had the privilege to come to this country as refugees realize that there is no place else to seek refuge. This is it. We have to make our last stand here. In my case, I was born in Poland before the Nazis invaded. "We had to leave," my parents said. It's a good thing we did, as there was no stopping Hitler in 1939.

There is a way to stop the "Establishment" and Clinton in the U.S.A., and they must be stopped. It's in our grasp to regain control over our own destiny. The first step in that process is to clean our house of corruption. In order to do that, we can not cover-up any transgressions by our leaders. If Clinton is guilty, he must be removed and punished, with his cohorts. If he is not, then he and they should welcome the light of day and the truth shed by it.

We will survive whatever happens. But question the quality of that survival. We cannot survive very well, if we live with his guilt, and let him off the hook. The fear of an international monetary crisis cannot control the situation. If we allow that, we will be worse off. Our own government doesn't respect us now. Who will then? Democracy in America will go down in history as the joke of the 20th Century.

We were once proud to be Americans. The conglomerate of international banks, once again, is trying to assert its absolute power over the fate of the United States and other countries. Let's show them that we are proud Americans and let's tell them that freedom is more important than money.

France just held it's election and over 80 percent of the registered voters went to the polls, voted Jaques Chirac, a conservative, into the presidency. A majority of the people of France have elected their president. We haven't had more than 50 percent of the registered voters show up for an election in my lifetime. Isn't it better to stop killing each other out of frustration and instead go and vote to change what's wrong? Isn't that the message of Oklahoma City, "Whitewater", Watergate, and the 20 percent that gave us President Clinton?

Part VI

A Solution:

In 1996 let's have a 90 percent, or better, voter turn out and let's vote for ordinary people like you and me, not stale "Party Puppets"! Vote out all incumbents--that's the revolution we need. We don't need superstars, the baseball strike proved that they only care about themselves. Those people are irrelevant today. We want Americans in office who care about their fellow Americans. They don't have to be Democrats or Republicans they can be Independents, or others, as long as they are Americans for America. We want congressman and senators who will do what we want them to do. That is the job of our representatives, be they in City Hall, in the State Capitols or in Washington D.C. Have you ever been paid for not doing your job? Why have we been paying these people for failing in their jobs? Fire them!!!

There are only 536 people elected to the House, the Senate and the White House; this small group controls two hundred fifty million Americans. We have allowed that small group of officials to financially devastate this great Country of ours. Why? The main reason is because we have two parties, the Republicans and the Democrats. Each has its own agenda, and that agenda does not include our well-being. It's like watching two prostitutes walking down the street. One is attempting to outdo the other in order to attract customers.

We can't afford to continue abusing our democracy in that manner. As an example, the two party system breeds corruption and prevents us from putting Clinton, and others, under the microscope of public scrutiny. Constant deals and constant favors between Democrats and Republicans, for their own survival, these "back scratching" deals are killing our nation. In the future, whomever we nominate to run for president or any other political office for that matter, must have verifiable references.

With computers, the Internet, etc..., someone ought to figure out a way to get credentials on all candidates who want to run, so we can scrutinize everyone before they are nominated. Our "leaders" once were exemplary in character and honesty. Today we can afford nothing less for president of the U.S.A. and on down the line to the local school board. If we can't find people like that, then democracy in this republic has failed.

The place to look for candidates is among honest, average Americans, who are not necessarily lawyers. Remember what William French Smith, the lawyer, did to the justice system, and the U.S. Constitution, which he swore to uphold. <u>Do not vote for lawyers</u>.

We have had an overabundance of lawyers in public office. As a result, we lost our common sense. Lawyers have very little of that, but they suffer from an abundance of self-indulgence as "law makers". Governing people in a complex society takes a lot more than just passing laws. We need a balance of women and men who are, artists, teachers, architects, engineers, butchers, grocers, librarians, writers, and other trades and professions. Vote in creative people, not law merchants. They had their turn, and they failed. Now they have to go back to the end of the line, and give others a chance.

The U.S. Constitution instructs and directs you and me to preserve democracy as it was intended to be preserved, through the ballot. That is our duty!

The immediate solution might be the merger of mainstream political parties, such as; the Republican Party, the Democratic Party, United We Stand for America, the Concord Coalition, the Libertarian Party, the Peace and Freedom Party into a new party, the "American Party" Don't worry about that being unconstitutional. Other parties will also form, that you can be sure of. There will be the Socialist Party, the Nazi or Neo-Nazi, the Communists or the Neo-Communists Parties, the Greens and others.

We have to unite mainstream American parties under one umbrella, not divide them into three or more parties. Just as government has to get smaller, the party system has to be reduced. We simply can't afford the other alternative.

This is a very complex suggestion and it needs a considerable amount of study. Certainly more than the limits of this book allow. The basic concept and the driving force must not be money, as it has always been in the past. We have to grow up about money. It's true, we can make more money here than anywhere else in the world. So what! Let's stop gloating about it like adolescent children.

Discipline is the mother's milk of a resiliency which makes this country strong. Resiliency, if nurtured carefully with hope, and less greed will get us through this crisis. That way we can continue taking care of the business of democracy, and it can last forever. That is our choice. "United we stand, divided we fall". Let's have one American Party and let's organize it ourselves. "Re-elect Nobody in '96" is the slogan to do that. If no Republicans or Democrats hold office in '96 and in 2000, that will do it. We will have eliminated both parties---put them out of existence.

Some additional suggestions are offered to help all of us start a dialogue among ourselves to resuscitate our Democracy. Let's assume....

The elected officials of the American Party would eventually vote in a "bloc", (just as the Republicans and Democrats now do). This will change and abolish once and for all the rivalry which now exists. By this suggestion, the American Party's only concern shall be for its members, not special interest groups. There will still be those of course, but there is no reason why any group should have preference over another.

What is causing inequality is money and the competition between the two parties for that "almighty buck". The result is chaotic to democracy and spawns a capitalistic take over for the benefit of an "Establishment".

Capitalism cannot and must not be equated with democracy. Free Enterprise yes, but it has to be protected from capitalism as it is being practiced in the U.S.A. There is no mention of capitalism in the U.S. Constitution.

Capitalism is greed and the worse kind of "whoredom". It has been touted as an antidote to Communism. It is not. Democracy is, and that is what America is all about. It's not a capitalist form of government, it is a Republic which has a democratic form of government driven by free enterprise.

The "American Party's" national platform should include, among others, the following suggestions:

> - There will be no ethnic distinctions made or labels attached to Americans, such as Afro, Asian, Latino, etc.... We are all Americans. Because we or our ancestors came from foreign lands is not a reason to label Americans with such ethnicity. Such labels cause a stratification of people in a democracy where everyone is considered to be equal. We acknowledge that under the laws of the Republic, all are equal, but we all realize that everyone is an individual, and as such, we are not technically equal.

> - The myth of equality ought to be dissolved. Just as some are taller than others, some are more gifted and more talented than others. That is a fact that we should acknowledge and accept. We also accept the fact that in a democracy it is imperative that the people who have more have a responsibility to take care of those who have less, and those that are better off have no right and will not be

71

allowed to take advantage of others. Those principals of fairness are the only valid test of human character and are the difference between a democracy's survival or it's eventual overthrow by a dissatisfied populace.

- We acknowledge the value of every individual human being and we acknowledge and respect the gifts that each one of us brings. Individual life is to be considered sacred. However, any woman has the right to terminate life in her womb. Her body is just as sacred, and she, not the government, controls it. There shall be no interference by government in that process and no government shall encourage abortion by providing taxpayer's money for such medical procedures. Once a life is delivered and dwells among us, it is then sacred and can only be extinguished if it has willfully extinguished the life of another. Religious considerations regarding this topic are up to the individual woman. Separation of Church and State must be preserved at all costs.

- Any and all portrayals of crime on television, the Internet and in the movies will be boycotted by the American Party its members will be encouraged not to pay for tickets in protest, as it is totally a needless exhibition of human depravity. Obviously promotion of depravity is not in the best interest of all Americans.

- The exploitation of perversion through the portrayal of sex acts shall not be allowed on television, the Internet, or any other government permitted medium.

- Columbia produces 80 percent of all cocaine and heroin in the world. A few years ago the Medelin Cartel was stopped. Now the Cali Cartel has been broken. A new one is already in place. It doesn't matter where or who supplies drugs. There will always be someone as long as there is a demand. The American Party must take the lead at home and abroad to wipe out the thirst for drugs and stamp out the supply. Perhaps it's time to call in the United States Marine Corps and really go to war on drug dealers, users and all gang members in our cities and abroad. Perhaps World War III is that, let's face it!!!

- The American Party will change the taxation laws on the federal level to provide for a uniform 15 percent income tax for individuals and corporations on every dollar of gross income. There shall be no deductions of any kind and no credits whatsoever. In addition, there shall be a 10 percent national sales tax on every sale in the country. Products or merchandise sold beyond our borders, but brought in to the U.S.A. for use here, shall all be subject to a 10 percent tax, based on retail value. The budget of the federal government will be geared to meet that and only that income.

There shall be no other fees paid by U.S. citizens to the government. Each year there shall be a 10 percent reserve of the government's gross income set aside for emergencies. Foreigners who want to live here will pay a 10% surcharge on their income, until they become citizens.

- A Social Security tax of 5 percent shall be paid by everyone over the age of 30, from which benefits will start to be paid at age 68. The Social Security System shall not be administered by Congress or any branch of the government. Funds shall be collected and administered by a separate, non-profit organization of retired persons, over 68 whose officers shall be selected by its members to a one time, two-year term.

- The Education Department shall be disbanded, as there is no need for such a department on the national level. The states will administer public education. There shall be no federal subsidies paid to the states for education.

- There shall be no foreign aid given to any sovereign country by the federal government. In the event a natural catastrophe occurs abroad, such as storms, earthquakes, etc..., a maximum of 10 percent per year from the National Emergency Fund may be used during any one year period to aid any and all foreign governments in helping their people survive. There shall be no exceptions. The Truman Doctrine shall be abolished, there shall be no intervention whatsoever by U.S. armed forces in the internal affairs of any foreign country.

- All foreign imports of products made abroad which are similar to and compete with products made in the U.S.A. shall be taxed at the port of entry. This tariff shall be equal to 10 percent of the proposed retail price of such products. All other trade shall not be restricted. The proceeds from such collections shall be part of the federal governments income.

- The National Endowment for the Arts is a most important institution to preserve the cultural heritage of creative expression in America, by Americans. That institution shall be renamed "The National Creativity Center". Its scope shall be enlarged to allow invention of products and technology, as well as the arts. It shall be funded by 1 percent of the federal income and matching grants from private sources, the sum total of those funds shall constitute it's annual budget.

- Medical costs shall be regulated by each state limiting what may be charged. There shall be no national health care programs. HMO's will be eliminated. All health care in the U.S.A. shall be non-profit, private delivery. There shall be no government facilities. County or state hospitals shall be privatized. What was known as Medicaid and Medicare shall be the responsibility of every state, starting in the year 2000. Health insurance shall be a non-profit institution, such as the new Social Security organization suggested above.

- All county governments, or their equivalent, shall be eliminated throughout all the states of the union by the year 2000. They are redundant, no longer relevant, and we cannot afford them. Functions administered by counties shall be divided between cities and states. All city governments in a regional area with abutting borders shall be combined to eliminate duplication of services and duplication of unnecessary costs. There shall be no minimum or maximum population limits on cities. Natural, not political, boundaries shall designate city limits. Lands in between, which are sparsely populated, shall be administered by the States.

- Environmental protection laws and regulations shall be re-written. The primary consideration of all such legislation shall be the well-being of the American citizens, nationally or regionally. Animal life and plant life shall not take precedence over human life. At the same time, animal life and plant life shall be protected as it has been. Land and water on this planet is the source of all life. Without clean land and water there is no possibility of life on Earth. Therefore, land and water shall be protected in the same manner and to the same degree as human life. As a result, all nuclear devices shall be collected inter-nationally and sent off into deep space to be banned forever from the planet. Anyone or any group, who continues to manufacture the nuclear devices, gets a one way ticket with the next load.

- The American Party shall advocate the following Political and election reforms:

- Term limits:

President	Two 4 year terms maximum
Senator	One 8 year term (no re-election)
Congressman	One 4 year term (no re-election)
Federal Judges	One 10 yr term (no re-election & no life terms)

(All Federal Judges are to be elected, as are State and Municipal Judges, not appointed.)

- Radio & Television time:

There shall be established a special radio and television channel whose sole function shall be to allow equal free time to all federal candidates running for office to present themselves to the voters. Weekly time slots shall be allocated to all candidates and shown regionally or nationally as called for. The states and cities shall be encouraged to develop similar channels locally and statewide. There shall be no "paid for" political advertising allowed on commercial and/or cable television, radio, or the Internet. This will constitute a separation of "networks & state", which is just as important as separation of "church & state".

- Newspaper and magazine advertising shall be free and equal to all candidates. Information about candidates disseminated by the print media shall be in the form of and more like news announcements in lieu of advertising and shall be labeled "Political Announcement".

- All campaigns shall be governed by a non-partisan, National & State Campaigning, Election Commissions to be created and administered by both past office holders and future candidates on a 50/50 rotation. Only a one, four year term of office in a lifetime shall be allowed on the National and State Campaign Commissions. "Professional Politicians" shall phase out into oblivion, starting with the 1996 election, and term limits shall be retroactive to that date.

- There shall be no Political Action Committees and no contributions, whatsoever, for political office of any kind, from individuals, business or other institutions of any kind. Money shall never again determine the success of a potential candidate or the outcome of legislation.

- The American Party shall nominate a number of screened and qualified candidates for each office in a primary election. Information on all candidates from birth to the present time shall be made available, free of charge, on the Internet, the print media, and by fax on demand from the National Campaign & Election Commission. In the event any such proposed candidate's background is found to be other than as reported, such candidate shall be withdrawn automatically, and without a hearing, from the election process permanently by the National Campaign & Election Commission.

- The final election shall be held between the two candidates who have the highest number of votes. Candidates from political parties other than the American Party may also appear on the final election ballot.

- Any elected official shall receive pay commensurate with what that person earned, as reported to the IRS, in the last calendar year before the election. There shall be a minimum base pay established so as not to punish or discourage low wage earners from holding office. There shall also be no maximum paid. Men and women who are highly paid should not be discouraged from serving their Country because of pay penalties. In addition, an equal amount of expense funds will be allocated for each office, based on a pro-rata share of constituents served.

- There shall be no federal subsidies to any free enterprise group, such as farm, wine, sugar subsidies, etc.... From now on, free enterprise must fend for itself in world markets. Any and all small business loans are a regional matter and shall be administered on a state-wide basis by state run SBA's.

- All other issues shall be resolved by a common sense consensus, with all priority in all decisions going to the individual taxpayer, who is, to put it bluntly, the only customer of government. The taxpayer owns the country and its government.

We are now ready to wipe the slate clean and live by the infinite wisdom of the Ten Commandments, God's laws, given to Moses on Mount Sinai three thousand years ago. In case you have forgotten what they legislate:

1. I am the Lord your God, you shall have no other gods before me.

2. Do not make idols and worship them. I, the Lord your God, am a jealous God, punishing the children for the sin of the father to the fourth generation of those who hate me, but showing love to all who love me and keep my commandments.

3. You shall not misuse the name of the Lord your God, for the Lord will not hold anyone guiltless who misuses his name.

4. Remember the Sabbath day by keeping it Holy. Six days you shall labor and do all your work, but on the seventh day is a Sabbath to the Lord your God. On it you shall not do any work, neither you, nor your son or daughter, nor your man servant or maidservant, nor your animals, nor the alien within our gates. For in six days the Lord made the heavens and the Earth, and the sea, and all that is in them, but he rested on the seventh day. Therefore, the Lord blessed the Sabbath day and made it Holy.

5. Honor your father and Mother, so that you may live long in this land the Lord your God is giving you.

6. You shall not murder.

7. You shall not commit adultery.

8. You shall not steal.

9. You shall not give false testimony against your neighbor.

10. You shall not covet (want) your neighbor's house. You shall not covet (lust for) your neighbor's wife, or (take away) his manservant, or maidservant, his ox or donkey, or anything that belongs to your neighbor.

Exodus 20, 1:18

Part VII

The List of Characters:

The following is a list of names involved in "Whitewater". These are the players and organizations provided for your easy reference. Use it when the hearings are on T.V. as a players roster is used on a sports program.

Whitewater Development Corp.

The New Republic	Campobello
Castle Grande	Park-on-Meter Co.
BBCI	Mena, Arkansas
London Sunday Telegram	Rose Law Firm
Irangate	Bank of Kingston
"Screw Worm"	"Jade Bridge"
"Centaur Rose"	Worthen Tower

Travelgate
The Resolution Trust Corp.
Arkansas Development Finance Authority
Madison Guarantee Savings & Loan
Capital Management Services, Inc.

President Bill Clinton	First Lady Hillary Clinton
Vince Foster	Jim McDougal
Steve Smith	Governor Jim Guy Tucker

Luther "Jerry" Parks
David Hale
Jim Blair
Robert Fiske
Jon Parnell Walker
Maggie Williams
Bill Shelton
Patsy Thomasson
Sheffield Nelson
Christopher Bond
William Casey
Beryl Anthony
Montgomery Riser
Ronald Rogers, D.D.S.
Barry Seal
John Cummings
Ronald Reagan
Kevin Ives
Famey Mallock
Keith Coney
Gregory Collins
Jeff Rhodes
Paul Wilcher
John A. Wilson
Jim Wilhite
Steven Dickson
William Barkley
Brian Hassey
L.J. Davis
Pete Marwick
Sally Perdue
Janet Reno

Jane Parks
Sgt. Clyde Steelman
Don Tyson
Bernard Nussbaum
Danny Ferguson
Paula Jones
Kathy Ferguson
Sgt. George Gonzales
William Sessions
Keith McKaskle
Ollie North
C. Victor Riser II
Herschel Friday
Ambrose E. Pritchard
Terry Read
Charles Black
William Barr
Don Henry
Virginia Kelley
Richard Winters
Jordan Ketelson
Danny Casolaro
Ed Willey
Paula Gober
Stanley Heard
Timothy Sabel
Scott Reynolds
Dan Lasater
Lawrence Walsh
Roger Clinton
Sally Jesse Raphael
L.D. Brown

84

Cliff Jackson	Henry O'Neill
Roger Perry	Lynn Davis
Buddy Young	Gwen Ifill
Gary Johnson	Gennifer Flowers
Jeremy Hedges	Wal-Mart
Tysons Chicken	Seth Ward
Webb Hubbell	Gary Parks
Neal T. Ainley	Bruce Lindsey
Herby Branscum, Jr.	Dean Paul
George Mitchell	Lloyd Bentsen
William J. Marks	John H. Haley
George Collins	James Lyons
Susan McDougal	William Kennedy, III
Roger Altman	Robert Palmer
Beverly Basset Schaffer	Chris Wade
George Stephanopoulos	Larry Paterson

Key Hearing figures who want Clinton out:

Robert Dole, Senator - R. Kansas
Newt Gingrich, Congressman - R. Georgia
Phil Gramm, Senator - R. Texas
Jesse Helms, Senator - R. N. Carolina
Pete Wilson, Governor - R. California
Alfonse M. D'Amato, Senator - R. New York
Jim Leach, Congressman - R. Iowa
Al Gore, Vice President - D. U.S.A.
Ross Perot, "I told you so." - U.S.A.

Part VIII

Epilogue:

The outcome of "The Whitewater Tidal Wave" will be clarified when we find out more about Vince Foster. Hillary Clinton is the most informed person in the U.S.A. on that subject. She knows more about Foster than does his wife. Their intimate relationship may have been just a drop in the bucket. There is reportedly a $50 million bank account in Switzerland in the name of Chelsea Jefferson. It supposedly got there via Vince Foster's frequent trips to Geneva and Zurich, which started during the time Mena was a drug running operation in the state of Arkansas. There are accusations that Governor Clinton extracted that amount from the Mena operators as his cut.

All we know now about Foster, so far:

> - Foster was an intimate confidant, friend and financial advisor to William Jefferson Clinton, his wife Hillary, and daughter Chelsea.
>
> - Foster was in possession of a round trip ticket to Geneva when he died.
>
> - Foster handled the Chelsea Jefferson "Clinton" bank account in Switzerland.

- Foster routed the money from Mena through Little Rock, the Fuji Bank, through Grand Cayman's tax free accounts, and to the safe haven of a secret Swiss bank account.

- Foster logged over a half million air miles on frequent flyer programs on Delta and other airlines, about which he didn't tell Lisa, his wife.

- Foster has a sister, Shelia Anthony, who is a top official at the Justice Department.

- Foster's tickets to Geneva and Zurich were sometimes purchased through the White House Travel Office. Records will show that he traveled on December 7, 1992, during the presidential transition period, to Switzerland for one day and then back to the U.S.A.

- Foster was scheduled to go to Switzerland again on July 8, 1993, and purchased that ticket on July 1, 1993, but he never made it.

- Foster flew before the election to the Orient, the Middle East, and to Switzerland many times. He traveled always in a category of discount fares reserved for federal contract operatives. Some say that he was a secret agent--, however, they are not certain who paid him. It's possible that he could have been a double agent.

- Foster was apparently implicated with the Bush administration, Caspar Weinberger, the CIA, and the Iran-Contra scandal.

- If Foster was murdered. The Fiske investigation was a fraud on the American voters. Kenneth Starr is following right in Fiske's footsteps. D'Amato is soft peddling. When Newt Gingrich's House Republicans get started with their hearings, things will happen. The Senate seems impotent. The House is full of mavericks, out for blood, who want to make a name for themselves. They are newly elected and had absolutely nothing to do with the Whitewater mess.

- Foster's murder will bring down the entire Clinton administration, including Vice President Gore.

The U.S. Constitution provides that the Speaker of the House is next in line. In that event, Newt Gingrich will stand for re-election in November 1996. As a result, many will consider him the savior of America and he will be re-elected in 2000. The "hype" will be; "for the good of the people who no longer trust the government, or attorneys for that matter".

Under the circumstances, that is the best chance we have for survival. The alternatives are too horrible to even contemplate; "what's his name", the old guy from Kansas, or General Powell, a military puppet dictator owned and trained by the establishment, or billionaire

Perot, a despotic egomaniac. For the Democrats, Lee Iacocca is a good bet in '96, or Michael Eisner, the "Mickey Mouse President", might be better. Eventually we will get over "The Whitewater Tidal Wave", but the U.S.A. will never be the same. America's slogan is: **"Re-elect Nobody in '96"**.

Please participate and write your opinion or use the prepared tear-out cards following to:

Senator Alfonse M. D'Amato
520 Hart Building
Washington, DC 20510

Congressman Jim Leach
2186 Rayburn Building
Washington, DC 20510

Pebble Beach Press, Ltd.
P.O. Box 1171
Pebble Beach, CA 93953

Each of your two Senators

&

to your congressional
representative.

We have also provided three bumper or window stickers, **"Re-elect Nobody in '96"**. You may simply put some rubber cement on these and stick them to the bumper of your car or in the rear window.

Dear Senator D'Amato & Congressman Leach,

I have read A.K. Karsky's "The Whitewater Tidal Wave" and if any part of it is true, we want President Clinton and Hillary to be charged with the offenses that you find they did commit. Secrecy has gone far enough, corrupt politics must be stopped. We trust you will put nothing above the sacred trust that the American People have placed in your hands, we elected you. No matter what happens, we want the truth out in the open. Yes, even if it means a global monetary crisis. The bankers are not your masters, the American people are. It's time to clean house. You can't cover up all that trash. Let's get rid of it.

Name _____

Address _____

City_____ State _____

Zip code _____ Phone Number _____

Please remember to send me a copy.
Thanks,

A.K. Karsky Pebble Beach Press, Ltd. P.O. Box 1171 Pebble Beach, CA 93953

Dear Senator D'Amato & Congressman Leach,

I have read A.K. Karsky's "The Whitewater Tidal Wave" and if any part of it is true, we want President Clinton and Hillary to be charged with the offenses that you find they did commit. Secrecy has gone far enough, corrupt politics must be stopped. We trust you will put nothing above the sacred trust that the American People have placed in your hands, we elected you. No matter what happens, we want the truth out in the open. Yes, even if it means a global monetary crisis. The bankers are not your masters, the American people are. It's time to clean house. You can't cover up all that trash. Let's get rid of it.

Name _____

Address _____

City_____ State _____

Zip code _____ Phone Number _____

Please remember to send me a copy.
Thanks,

A.K. Karsky Pebble Beach Press, Ltd. P.O. Box 1171 Pebble Beach, CA 93953

"Re-elect nobody in '96"

Copyright © Pebble Beach Press, Ltd.

From: _____   **Place**

      _____   **Stamp**

      _____   **Here**

To: Senator Alfonse M. D'Amato
520 Hart Building
Washington, DC 20510

From: _____   **Place**

      _____   **Stamp**

      _____   **Here**

To: Congressman Jim Leach
2186 Rayburn Building
Washington, DC 20515

Dear Senator D'Amato & Congressman Leach,

I have read A.K. Karsky's "The Whitewater Tidal Wave" and if any part of it is true, we want President Clinton and Hillary to be charged with the offenses that you find they did commit. Secrecy has gone far enough, corrupt politics must be stopped. We trust you will put nothing above the sacred trust that the American People have placed in your hands, we elected you. No matter what happens, we want the truth out in the open. Yes, even if it means a global monetary crisis. The bankers are not your masters, the American people are. It's time to clean house. You can't cover up all that trash. Let's get rid of it.

Name _____

Address _____

City_____ State _____

Zip code _____ Phone Number _____

Please remember to send me a copy.
Thanks,

A.K. Karsky Pebble Beach Press, Ltd. P.O. Box 1171 Pebble Beach, CA 93953

Dear Senator,

I have read A.K. Karsky's "The Whitewater Tidal Wave" and if any part of it is true, we want President Clinton and Hillary to be charged with the offenses that you find they did commit. Secrecy has gone far enough, corrupt politics must be stopped. We trust you will put nothing above the sacred trust that the American People have placed in your hands, we elected you. No matter what happens, we want the truth out in the open. Yes, even if it means a global monetary crisis. The bankers are not your masters, the American people are. It's time to clean house. You can't cover up all that trash. Let's get rid of it.

Name _____

Address _____

City_____ State _____

Zip code _____ Phone Number _____

Please remember to send me a copy.
Thanks,

A.K. Karsky Pebble Beach Press, Ltd. P.O. Box 1171 Pebble Beach, CA 93953

"Re-elect nobody in '96"

Copyright © Pebble Beach Press, Ltd.

From: _____

_____

_____

Place
Stamp
Here

To: Pebble Beach Press, Ltd.
P.O. Box 1171
Pebble Beach, CA 93953

From: _____

_____

_____

Place
Stamp
Here

To: Senator

Dear Senator,

I have read A.K. Karsky's "The Whitewater Tidal Wave" and if any part of it is true, we want President Clinton and Hillary to be charged with the offenses that you find they did commit. Secrecy has gone far enough, corrupt politics must be stopped. We trust you will put nothing above the sacred trust that the American People have placed in your hands, we elected you. No matter what happens, we want the truth out in the open. Yes, even if it means a global monetary crisis. The bankers are not your masters, the American people are. It's time to clean house. You can't cover up all that trash. Let's get rid of it.

Name _____

Address _____

City_____ State _____

Zip code _____ Phone Number _____

Please remember to send me a copy.
Thanks,

A.K. Karsky Pebble Beach Press, Ltd.   P.O. Box 1171   Pebble Beach, CA 93953

Dear Representative,

I have read A.K. Karsky's "The Whitewater Tidal Wave" and if any part of it is true, we want President Clinton and Hillary to be charged with the offenses that you find they did commit. Secrecy has gone far enough, corrupt politics must be stopped. We trust you will put nothing above the sacred trust that the American People have placed in your hands, we elected you. No matter what happens, we want the truth out in the open. Yes, even if it means a global monetary crisis. The bankers are not your masters, the American people are. It's time to clean house. You can't cover up all that trash. Let's get rid of It.

Name _____

Address _____

City_____ State _____

Zip code _____ Phone Number _____

Please remember to send me a copy.
Thanks,

A.K. Karsky Pebble Beach Press, Ltd.   P.O. Box 1171   Pebble Beach, CA 93953

"Re-elect nobody in '96"

Copyright © Pebble Beach Press, Ltd.

From: _____

_____

_____

Place
Stamp
Here

To: Senator

From: _____

_____

_____

Place
Stamp
Here

To:Representative